D0147478

OCEANS IN WORLD HISTORY

OCEANS IN WORLD HISTORY

RAINER F. BUSCHMANN

California State University Channel Islands

Boston   Burr Ridge, IL   Dubuque, IA   Madison, WI   New York
San Francisco   St. Louis   Bangkok   Bogotá   Caracas   Kuala Lumpur
Lisbon   London   Madrid   Mexico City   Milan   Montreal   New Delhi
Santiago   Seoul   Singapore   Sydney   Taipei   Toronto

Higher Education

OCEANS IN WORLD HISTORY

Published by McGraw-Hill, an imprint of The McGraw-Hill Companies, Inc., 1221 Avenue of the Americas, New York, NY 10020. Copyright © 2007. All rights reserved. No part of this publication may be reproduced or distributed in any form or by any means, or stored in a database or retrieval system, without the prior written consent of The McGraw-Hill Companies, Inc., including, but not limited to, in any network or other electronic storage or transmission, or broadcast for distance learning.

This book is printed on acid-free paper.

1 2 3 4 5 6 7 8 9 0 DOC/DOC 0 9 8 7 6

ISBN-13: 978-0-07-301903-1
ISBN-10: 0-07-301903-8

Editor in Chief: *Emily Barrosse*
Publisher: *Lyn Uhl*
Senior Sponsoring Editor: *Jon-David Hague*
Editorial Coordinator: *Sora Kim*
Production Service: *Val Heffernan, Carlisle Publishing Services*
Cover Design: *Srdjan Savanovic*
Senior Production Supervisor: *Rich DeVitto*
Composition: *10/13 Palatino by Carlisle Publishing Services*
Printing: *45# New Era Matte, R. R. Donnelley & Sons*

Library of Congress Cataloging-in-Publication Data

Buschmann, Rainer F.
    Oceans of world history / Rainer F. Buschmann.--1st ed.
      p. c.
    Includes bibliographical references and index.
    ISBN 0-07-301903-8
    1. Ocean and civilization. 2. Civilization--History. 3. World history.
  4 .Ocean--History. 5. Globalization. I. Title.
CB465.B87 2007
909'.09--dc22

                                        2006048126

www.mhhe.com

For the student participants in my
Themes in World History Class
(Oceans of World History)

❰ TABLE OF CONTENTS ❱

A NOTE FROM
THE SERIES EDITORS

World history has come of age. No longer regarded as a task simply for amateurs or philosophers, it has become an integral part of the historical profession, and one of its most exciting and innovative fields of study. At the level of scholarship, a growing tide of books, articles, and conferences continues to enlarge our understanding of the many and intersecting journeys of humankind, framed in global terms. At the level of teaching, more and more secondary schools as well as colleges and universities now offer, and sometimes require, world history of their students. One of the prominent features of the world history movement has been the unusually close association of its scholarly and its teaching wings. Teachers at all levels have participated with university-based scholars in the development of this new field.

The McGraw-Hill series—Explorations in World History—operates at this intersection of scholarship and teaching. It seeks to convey the results of recent research in world history in a form wholly accessible to beginning students. It also provides a pedagogical alternative to or supplement for the large and inclusive core textbooks that are features of so many world history courses. Each volume in the series focuses briefly on a particular theme, set in a global and comparative context. And each of them is "open-ended," raising questions and drawing students into the larger issues that animate world history.

Among the major themes of world history is that of cross-cultural interaction. Rainer Buschmann's *Oceans in World History* presents an innovative way of thinking about that theme, centered on the notion that the world's oceans have been highways of communication and exchange rather than simply barriers to human connection. Professor Buschmann shows clearly that in the Indian, Atlantic, and Pacific oceans, human communities have long been embedded in networks of transregional interaction that have decisively shaped their historical development. His accounts include the early oceanic migrations of Austronesian-speaking peoples, the making of an Indian Ocean commercial and cultural world, the creation of interacting Atlantic and Pacific webs in the context of European expansion, and the role of oceans in the globalizing processes of recent centuries. While many world history books tell the stories of particular civilizations, *Oceans in World History* provides an alternative sea-based prism through which we can see the human journey in a unique and compelling fashion.

Robert Strayer
Kevin Reilly

◉ PREFACE ◉

A general assumption holds that liquid surfaces make for imprecise history due to the obvious absence of landmarks. Clearly delineated borders, after all, are manifestations of nation-states that figure prominently in historical discussions. At the same time, however, world historians are trying to transcend individual national histories to bring about a growing global awareness. In the search for larger units of analysis, world historians working in tandem with geographers have recognized the importance of ocean basins. To be sure, the ocean's watery expenses lack such markers as mountains, streams, and valleys to which we are accustomed. Similarly, the oceans' seemingly never-ending vastness initially appears as a natural boundary separating rather than uniting societies. Yet, at the same time, humans started to traverse oceans as early as two millennia before the start of the Common Era. Some of these individuals (e.g., Columbus and Cook) are well known, whereas others (Austronesian mariners) have recently emerged from the margins of history. Despite obvious differences and sometimes brutal consequences of their journeys, they nevertheless shared a conceptual recognition that the oceans' waters united rather than divided people. Such recognition is central to the present text.

Oceans in World History explores the global interconnections created by the exploration and charting of the world's largest oceans: the Atlantic, Indian, and Pacific. The book is divided into four main chapters. The first three are devoted to the historical exploration of the aforementioned oceans, and the last chapter explores the global integration of these oceans after 1800. The book is inspired by maritime history's emphasis on the relationship between seafaring and technological change. Its main purpose, however, is in tracing the cultural, demographic, and socioeconomic factors flowing from the integration of individual ocean basins. In this sense, the work remains closely tied to world historical investigations.

HOW TO USE THIS BOOK

Oceans in World History serves as a complementary text for introductory world history and world civilization classes. Its topics, however, resonate with an ever-growing title of maritime history courses and should thus find application within these classes as well. Students and instructors alike are encouraged to consider oceans as a convenient lens to explore the unfolding of world history. The work is far from exhaustive, and its suggestive nature affords great flexibility in the classroom. Each chapter begins with a **Getting Started** section that previews major questions emerging from the reading. Every chapter is followed by an annotated list of **Suggested Readings** highlighting the sources of information I have employed and providing starting points for further inquiries into individual topics.

A NOTE ON SPELLING

Transliteration of Chinese terms and proper names follows the *pinyin* system. Scholarly conventions govern transliterations of terms and names in other languages.

ACKNOWLEDGMENTS

My gratitude goes out to three individuals at California State University Channel Islands who went above and beyond in helping me with this book: David D'Amore assisted with the historical research, Izabela Betlinska provided expertise in the selection and improvement of maps and images, and Shannon Farley invested many hours in the editing of the chapters. Their assistance was made possible through a title of generous Channel Islands Faculty Development Grants, including the Martin V. Smith Faculty Innovation and Excellence Award. The grants also provided much-needed release time for the completion of the current project. Nian-Sheng Huang, Chair of the History Program and outstanding teacher-scholar, understood that scheduling is an intricate component of academic success. Another prominent historian at Channel Islands, Frank Barajas, never failed to provide stimulating discussions on the historicity of oceans. Kevin Volkan, my colleague in the Psychology Program, introduced me to important psychological dimensions of Asian cultures and aquatic consciousness.

A heartfelt thank you goes out to Jerry H. Bentley, who as advisor and mentor not only inspired the topic but also introduced me to the excellent editors of the McGraw-Hill series: Robert Strayer and Kevin Reilly. Bob has been supportive in the development of this text, reading countless drafts and offering constructive suggestions for improvement, and Kevin has provided guidance when needed. I would also very much like to thank two reviewers: Joshua Rosenthal from SUNY-Oneonta and Jaime Dunlop from Olivet College, who with great care read through the entire manuscript and whose comments greatly improved the final work.

I am grateful to my wife, Cèline Dauverd, who not only took time away from her dissertation research and writing to look through many of these chapters but facilitated the conclusion of this work through unwavering support.

Finally, thank you to my students who have patiently listened to the original ideas for this book and whose discussions stimulated many ways of developing the final product. I dedicate this book to them in recognition of their patience and dedication.

OCEANS IN WORLD
HISTORY

INTRODUCTION

OCEANS AND WORLD HISTORY

CHAPTER OUTLINE

The Big History of Oceans

The Historical Long-Term Cycles of Oceans

TIMELINE

4.6 billion years ago	Earth's formation
4 billion years ago	Vapor liquefied as water (through either comets or outgassing) to create oceans
200 million years ago	Breakup of Pangea (single landmass)
150 million years ago	Separation of Pangea into Laurasia and Godwana reveals the Pacific and Central Atlantic Oceans
94 million years ago	Further breakup of Laurasia and Godwana reveals North and South Atlantic
40 million years ago	Further plate tectonics reveals the Indian Ocean
20 million years ago	The Red Sea
2.5 million years ago	*Homo erectus* emerges
100,000 years ago	Anatomically modern humans emerge

Roughly 70 percent of the earth's surface is covered by water, and yet oceans have received only scant historical attention. As the historical discipline has developed into a bona fide academic endeavor, the nation-state has remained at the center of analysis. Only in more recent decades have historians developed a more global outlook; and even then, practitioners often unwittingly conceived of oceans as vast empty liquid spaces that obstructed rather than furthered human development. Nothing could be further from the truth. As the earth's oceans and seas have been explored through the natural sciences, awareness has grown of the oceans' important role in the earth's physical and historical development. Recently, historians combined physical and historical development in an approach called "Big History." Simply put, big historians contextualize human existence against the vast historical development of our planet.

THE BIG HISTORY OF OCEANS

There are two competing views on the origins of the world's oceans. The older version suggests that water feeding the oceans originated in the earth's interior and was transported to the surface by volcanic activity. More recently, this "internal" view has been complemented by an "exter-

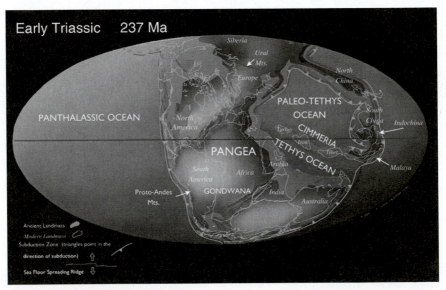

FIGURE I-1A   BIRTH OF OCEANS
Source: Used with permission from An Introduction to the World's Oceans (8th ed.), by Keith Sverdrup, Alyn C. Duxbury, and Alison B. Duxbury. Copyright 2004 by McGraw-Hill.

nal" version. Atmospheric scientists argue that small icy comets release vapor as they disintegrate upon collision with the outer atmosphere of our planet. Although the average mass of these comets is a little more than 20 pounds, rendering them invisible to the naked eye, it is estimated that almost 10 million of them reach the earth every year. These comets, together with the volcanic activity discussed earlier, significantly fuel the oceans' water supply.

Oceans, much like continents, are ever-evolving features. The process contributing to their movements is one generally described as plate tectonics. This course of action results from the fragmentation and movement of the earth's outer shell. Roughly 250 million years ago all continents were united in a gigantic geographical feature known as Pangaea. The waters surrounding this supercontinent fueled mostly the ocean that later became known as the Pacific. By about 200 million years ago, Pangaea broke apart, revealing two new continents, Laurasia on the northern hemisphere and Godwana on the southern hemisphere. As these two features continued to separate over the next 50 million years, during the time of the dinosaurs or the late Jurassic, the central Atlantic Ocean began to emerge. The southern Atlantic Ocean emerged by about 135 million years ago as the South American and African continents drifted further apart. The northern and southern Atlantic linked shortly after 100 million years ago. The last ocean to

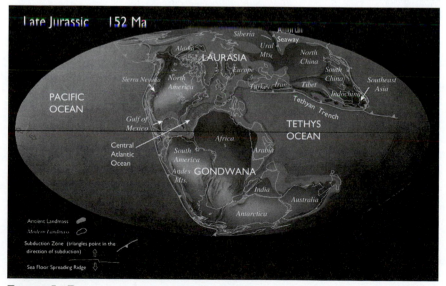

FIGURE I-1B

reveal itself was the Indian, emerging by about 60 million years ago. The last liquid feature to be created was the Red Sea, which emerged when the Arabian Peninsula moved away from the African continent. The intense forces pulling apart continents continue to affect the contemporary world. In December of 2004, a vast seaquake off the island of Sumatra (Indonesia) released a gigantic tsunami (Japanese for harbor wave) that caused massive devastation, with an estimated 250,000 lives lost.

THE HISTORICAL LONG-TERM CYCLES OF OCEANS

In 1949, a French historian by the name of Fernand Braudel provided an appropriate model to assess the oceans' impact on human existence on a slightly smaller scale than big historians use. Writing about the Mediterranean Sea, Braudel argued for an assessment of the *longue dureé* (French for "long duration"), long-term physical, economic, and cultural cycles that determined human development along the Mediterranean shores.

In the physical realm, oceans figure as giant thermostats absorbing and slowly surrendering heat to the surrounding land surfaces. This function has an important influence on global climates, providing for cooler summers and milder winters for coastal regions and their adjacent territories. The interplay between oceans, continents, and the earth's atmosphere significantly influences the establishment of currents, which in turn has affected human development globally. Four major factors establish the flow of the oceans' waters. First, and perhaps most obvious, are winds, which propel the upper water layers. Second is the influence of sun rays that heat water around the equator and circulate it to the earth's poles. Third, differential salt contents around the earth contribute to differential density of the water. Although salt, in all its chemical manifestations, amounts to less than 3 percent of the oceans' water, even smaller elevations of salt content affect water density, which in turn affects its circulation. The sun and the amount of precipitation are the main influences in this regard. The planet's tropical zones generally experience frequent rainfall, which lowers water density. Subtropical zones, on the other hand, experience less rain, and the frequent sunshine contributes to evaporation, thus increasing the density. Generally speaking, greater density prevents, while lesser density aids, water circulation. The last factor is the so-called Coriolis force. Discovered by a French mathematician in the 1800s, this force accounts for the deviating influences of the earth's rotation. The Coriolis force influences direction and velocity of ocean currents.

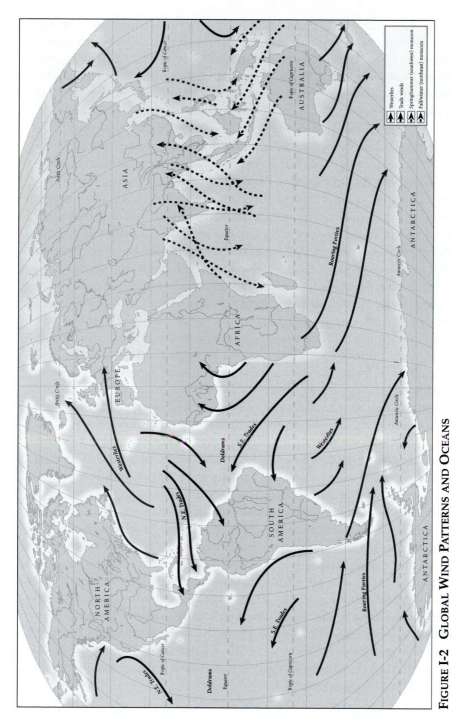

FIGURE I-2 GLOBAL WIND PATTERNS AND OCEANS

Source: Used with permission from Traditions and Encounters (2nd ed.), by Jerry H. Bentley and Herbert F. Ziegler. Copyright 2002 by McGraw-Hill.

Currents and winds figure prominently in human economic cycles. Maps frequently depict oceans as lifeless entities that separate animated continents. Geographical features dotting "terra firma," such as mountains and canyons, are all too often absent from oceans. Such representations are again distortions, as oceans and seas hold the highest mountains and deepest trenches.

Oceans also teem with movement. Scientists and, most recently, historians argue that the ocean currents are similar to rivers. Just as rivers that traverse continents served as major arteries of exploration and exchange prior to the introduction of steam and rail, so too did ocean currents, aided by constant wind directions, provide major connections during the Age of Sail. Early human societies quickly realized that river, sea, and ocean trade was far more economical than the overland equivalent. Ships could carry greater loads than beasts of burden, whether horses or camels, and did so at greater speed. Although shipwrecks were unfortunately frequent, a vessel's swiftness and carrying capacity outweighed any potential dangers. Once ocean currents and winds were mastered—a task that took the better part of centuries—oceans turned into frequently used highways. The mastery of the oceans' movements provided an important stimulus for technological advancement. Hull construction, sail shapes, and nautical instruments became vital steps in this process.

Long-distance trade also had a tremendous cultural impact on the societies living along the world oceans' shores. As they traveled across the oceans, humans took with them precious trade items frequently available in abundance at their point of departure, but much sought after at their point of arrival. Ranking alongside trade items in importance were ideas, in particular religious outlooks. Their interchange along ocean trade routes had a tremendous impact on world history. Pathogens, or diseases, were equally important, eradicating indigenous populations all over the world who lacked immunity to the imported diseases.

This book is a global history of oceans with a focus on their role in the development of human societies. Geographers have identified five major oceans—Arctic, Atlantic, Indian, Pacific, and Southern—three of which figure prominently in this work. The Arctic and Southern oceans find little mention in the pages that follow. While the Arctic is inhabited, it is permanently covered in ice, and most of the area of the Southern Ocean is not inhabited. Also, the history of the Arctic and Southern oceans' discovery and charting is more recent.

While on one hand, oceans may not lend themselves to the common 1500 CE division separating most world history classes, they do nevertheless provide important chronological and geographical accounts for students of world history. However imperfect, the chronological framework of oceans is applicable to most world history courses. The book opens with a historical treatment of the Indian Ocean, whose weather systems, controlled by seasonal monsoon winds, allowed for long-distance voyaging initiated roughly 3,000 years ago. This chapter pays special attention to the exchange of luxury items developed in the bordering regions of Africa and Asia. Similarly, the spread of global religions, in particular Buddhism, Hinduism, and Islam, finds detailed treatment here. Central to our discussion of the Indian Ocean is the time period of 700 to 1500 CE. This involves the development of Islam among the trade routes of the Indian Ocean and the opening of Chinese markets during the Tang Dynasty. The chapter closes with the arrival of the Portuguese mariners in the region.

At the same time that Europeans entered long-established patterns of Indian Ocean commerce, they also began to fashion the Atlantic Ocean as an arena of interaction. The exploration of this ocean in itself did not originate until 1500 CE, as Arabs, Phoenicians, and Vikings ventured beyond the Mediterranean and North seas to encounter, for brief periods of time, societies in North America and sub-Saharan Africa. Sustained contacts, however, emerged as Genoese, Portuguese, and Spanish explored the system of currents governing the Atlantic Ocean. The transatlantic voyage of the Genoese Christopher Columbus is frequently regarded as a major transition in world history. He initiated the so-called Columbian exchange, or an exchange of animals, diseases, plants, peoples, and ideas between what is commonly designated as the "Old World" (Africa, Asia, and Europe) and the "New World" (North and South America). The Atlantic chapter concludes with the spread of revolutions across the ocean, taking the reader to the year 1820.

The Pacific Ocean, presented in the third chapter, is the largest of the oceans featured in this work. Chronologically speaking, the Pacific settlement can be divided into two well-defined periods. The initial Austronesian settlement from Asian shores originated during the last ice age and concluded somewhere around 1000 CE, with a large number of two-way voyages following after this date. The second expansion followed in the 1500s with the European expansion into the Indian Ocean and from the newly contacted Americas. This chapter highlights the important economic and cultural interchanges that would link Asians, Europeans, and Pacific Islanders from the 1600s to the early decades of the 1800s.

The last chapter highlights the significance of the world's oceans over the last two centuries. The introduction of steam revolutionized ship travel and consequently increased the volume in passenger and commodity travel. Similarly, the steam revolution aided the expansion of Euro-American imperial power that would soon reach across the globe. The oceans, especially the Atlantic and the Pacific, became important battlefields during the last two global wars. At the same time, however, ocean connections created different international consciousnesses that linked Africans, socialists, and women. As oceans decreased in importance in passenger travel in the second half of the 1900s, their importance in commodity transportation increased exponentially. By the end of the twentieth century, humans emerged as a major threat to ecosystems of the world's oceans. The concluding pages of this work are devoted to this important topic.

SUGGESTED READINGS

For an accessible introduction to oceanography and the physical geography of oceans, consult Keith Sverdrup, Alyn C. Duxbury, and Alison B. Duxbury, *An Introduction to the World's Oceans,* 8th ed. (Boston: McGraw-Hill Higher Education, 2004). David Christian has just written a concise and illuminating work on big history, entitled *Maps of Time: An Introduction to Big History* (Los Angeles: University of California Press, 2004). The classical work on defining sea and ocean spaces as valid categories of historical analysis remains Fernand Braudel's *The Mediterranean and the Mediterranean World in the Age of Philip II,* 3 vols. (University of California Press, 1996 [1949]). Philip de Souza, *Seafaring and Civilization: Maritime Perspectives on World History* (London: Profile Books, 2001) provides a good introduction to the economic, religious, and technological aspects of seaward expansion mostly from a Western perspective. A novel critique of the historical definition of the earth's continents can be found in Martin Lewis and Kären Wigen's *The Myth of Continents: A Critique of Metageography* (Los Angeles: University of California Press, 1997). The same authors propose an alternative "Ocean centered" view of the world in a collection of essays entitled "Oceans Connect" in *The Geographical Review* 89 (1999). Consult here in particular the essay by Jerry Bentley, "Sea and Ocean Basins as Framework for Historical Analysis." Another important starting point is Rainer F. Buschmann's "Oceans of World History: Delineating Aquacentric Views in the Global Past" *History Compass* 2 (2004) WD 68, pp. 1–9. Two recent collections of essays should also be mentioned: Bernhard Klein and Gesa Mackenthun have edited *Sea Changes: Historicizing the Ocean* (New York: Routledge, 2004). Their collection on the hidden histories of the Atlantic and Pacific oceans emphasizes neglected components of class and gender as well as non-European actors. Daniel Finamore's *Maritime History as World History* (Gainesville: University Press of Florida, 2004) brings together an important set of essays that highlight the contributions of maritime historians to world history.

CHAPTER ONE TIMELINE

1000 BCE	Monsoon system decoded by Indian Ocean mariners
600–200 BCE	Spread of Hinduism and Buddhism via Indian Ocean
100–300 CE	Greco-Roman ventures into the Red and Arabian Seas
600 CE	Srivijaya emerges as a powerful state in Southeast Asia
650–800 CE	Rise of Islam stimulates maritime exchange
618–1279 CE	Tang and Song dynasties facilitate trade exchanges
1000 CE	Swahili city-states dominate maritime exchanges along the eastern shores of Africa
1400s	With the rise of Melaka, Islam gains a permanent foothold in insular Southeast Asia
1405–33	Zheng He leads seven expeditions to the Indian Ocean
1497–99	Vasco da Gama rounds Africa and enters the Indian Ocean

 CHAPTER ONE

THE INDIAN OCEAN: A FIRST MARITIME CROSSROADS

GETTING STARTED ON CHAPTER ONE: What atmospheric conditions determined sailing patterns in the Indian Ocean world? What factors facilitated the integration of the Indian Ocean world? How did the emergence of global religions, especially Islam, impact the region? What role did China's dynasties play in the Indian Ocean? How was the region experienced and depicted by travelers? What prompted the Portuguese expansion into the area?

CHAPTER OUTLINE

INTRODUCTION

The Indian Ocean is perhaps the best point of departure for an ocean-based world history. For the past 4,000 years, it has served as an important zone of interaction among societies from Africa, Asia, and Europe. Along the shores of the Indian Ocean an important cosmopolitan culture emerged, one that favored trade and exchange and shared many of the major world religions (most importantly Buddhism, Hinduism, and Islam). From about 2500 BCE to about 600 CE, the Mediterranean Sea and the island world of Southeast Asia emerged as commercially integrated regions. Human expansion outward from these regions brought integration to the Indian Ocean world, with the South Asian sub-continent playing a central role in this process. Then in the seventh century CE two important events altered the shape of the Indian Ocean world: the emergence of the Islamic faith in 622 CE and the establishment of the Tang Dynasty in China in 618 CE. The arrival of the Europeans in the 1500s marked yet another important phase in the history of the Indian Ocean world.

THE INDIAN OCEAN IN ANTIQUITY

The Indian Ocean is the world's third largest ocean, encompassing a surface of approximately 26 million square miles (67 million square kilometers). Seen from an earlier outlined "Big History" perspective, the Indian Ocean is the youngest discussed in the volume. The outline of this ocean did not emerge until about 60 million years ago. Some of its features, most prominently the Red Sea, did not emerge until 20 million years ago. In terms of world history the Indian Ocean witnessed a slow integration of huge geographical areas. The South Asian subcontinent stood at the center of a maritime trade network and served as an important terminus for trade emanating from the Mediterranean to the west and Southeast and East Asia to the east. The emerging sea routes ranging from the Persian Gulf and the Red Sea all the way to the South China Sea were some of the largest in history. It was not until the 1500s, with the European expansion, that the length of these routes was surpassed.

The Indian Ocean comprises a number of separate regions. The Red Sea and the Persian Gulf both lead to an area commonly known as the Arabian Sea, stretching from the Somali Coast and the Horn of Africa to the West Coast of India (better known as the Malabar Coast). The eastern part of the South Asian subcontinent (known as the Coromandel Coast) leads to the Bay of Bengal, which connects to Southeast Asia. The Strait of Melacca (leading through the Malay Peninsula and the Island of Sumatra) connects Southeast Asia to the South China Sea and thus to East Asia. Although the South China Sea is technically considered part of the Pacific Ocean, it is of great importance to the Indian Ocean world and is therefore included here.

The Indian Ocean differs from its Atlantic and Pacific counterparts in that most of its watery expanses lie south of the equator. This fact contributes to interesting climatic patterns, that, due to their seasonal winds, are commonly known as the monsoons.

The decoding of the monsoon wind patterns probably occurred during the first millennium BCE, which also witnessed the consolidation of strong states and empires along the shores of the Indian Ocean. If the monsoons provided the engine for increasing cultural and economic exchange, the uneven distribution of resources along the Indian Ocean rim provided incentives for that exchange. The monsoons not only provided winds, but also determined climatic influences and precipitation. Generally speaking, dryer regions planted grains, while rice cultivation became the preferred crop in wetter areas. Rice could be stored considerably longer than grains

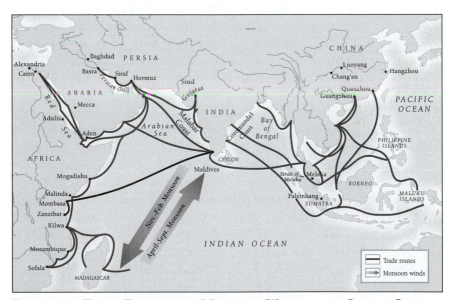

FIGURE 1-1 TRADE ROUTES AND MONSOON WINDS IN THE INDIAN OCEAN
Source: Used with permission from Traditions and Encounters (2nd ed.), by Jerry H. Bentley and Herbert F. Ziegler. Copyright 2002 by McGraw-Hill.

and became a major export item. While it is certainly true that ancient societies were more self-sufficient than contemporary nations, their degree
of economic independence has frequently been overestimated, and trade
for bare necessities was commonplace in many regions along the Indian
Ocean. Added to this was the unequal distribution of metals. This was particularly true for copper and tin, which were amalgamated to produce
bronze implements for the constructive endeavors of agriculture or the de-
structive forces of war. Thus the common designation of the Indian Ocean
exchange as one of luxury items, strengthened by the colorful accounts of
such epics as *One Thousand and One Nights* (a popular collection of tales
that includes Aladdin, Sindbad the voyager, and Ali-Baba and the forty
thieves), does not provide a wholly accurate picture. The exchange is probably better characterized as one that included both precious items and necessities, with luxury items usually taking longer trade routes than
common staples. Archaeologists suggests that rice and other food crops
may very well have been the reason behind the many shorter voyages, that
made up much of the Indian Ocean's rhythms. Historians argue that such
smaller ventures rather than long-distance trade accounted for the
longevity of the region's economic exchange. Similarly, what may be considered luxury in one place may have been a staple in another. A lengthy
voyage and increasing demand may have transformed an item into a desirable and ultimately expensive commodity. Cowry shells, for example,
originated in the Maldives, a chain of coral atolls just off the coast of India.
While they were of little value in the islands themselves, their durable consistency and relative low weight made them a much desired exchange currency around the Indian Ocean. Europeans even adopted this currency
when dealing with West African trading partners in the transatlantic slave
trade (see chapter 2).

Initial voyages into the Indian Ocean had two points of departure: the
island world of Southeast Asia and the great river civilizations of Egypt,
the Indus Valley, and Mesopotamia. The first thrust into the Indian Ocean
originated from river valley civilizations adjacent to the Mediterranean
Sea. Generally speaking, none of these voyages covered more than a few
hundred miles, and they were made within reach of the shores of the Red
Sea. Nevertheless, these shores were surrounded by reefs and shoals that
made navigation a difficult affair. Initially, maritime trade in the western
regions was a distant second to overland exchange, which received a powerful boost from the domestication of the camel 4,000 years ago. Yet from
reed-constructed river fishing boats eventually developed planked boats,
which in the Mediterranean Sea carried oars as well as sails. The Sumeri-

ans of Mesopotamia, for instance, used the mouths of the Tigris and Eu-
phrates rivers to sail through the Persian Gulf to the delta of the Indus
River. Trade goods from both regions abound in archaeological records,
and some researchers suggest that the yet to be deciphered Indus Valley
script may have been inspired by Mesopotamian cuneiform. In about 2500
BCE, the Sumerians were joined by the Egyptians, who sailed through the
Red Sea to the Indian Ocean to exchange manufactured goods for gold,
ivory, and slaves in Yemen, Ethiopia, and Somalia (possibly the area
known as Punt). It was the Egyptians who invited other Levantine peoples
to partake in this exchange. The most famous of these were the Phoenicians, who hailed from modern-day Lebanon. They not only improved
shipping technology by adding a sharp prow to their vessels, but also established themselves as traders in their own right. The Phoenicians controlled commodity exchanges in much of the Mediterranean and the Red
Sea. Greeks and Persians soon broke the Phoenician stranglehold over
Mediterranean trade and fought a protracted set of wars that ended with
Alexander the Great's conquest of the Persian Empire in 331 BCE. His
short-lived imperial presence in the Persian Gulf only increased the volume of trade and opened up new exchanges between India and the
Mediterranean region.

A different set of voyages emerged out of the thousands of islands that
make up Indonesia today. This great variety of islands supplied a multi-
tude of sheltered environments that provided optimal trial-and-error conditions to develop sturdy crafts and nautical techniques. It was somewhere
during the first millennium BCE that canoes stabilized by shaped logs
known as outriggers carried so-called Austronesian-speaking people
across the Indian Ocean to the island of Madagascar, whose inhabitants
still speak several Austronesian languages, especially Malagasy, as a result. These Austronesian sailors also brought with them bananas, Asian
yams, and taro, which they introduced to the island of Madagascar. The
presence of such crops in East Africa indicates a diffusion from Madagascar. Unlike the case in Madagascar, however, this contact had no linguistic
repercussion, as no Austronesian language can be found on the African
continent. The introduced plants, on the other hand, enriched the African
diet for generations. The same Austronesians who braved the Indian
Ocean to reach Madagascar also became ancestors to the Pacific Islanders
(see chapter 3) and established contact with the South Asian subcontinent.
India went on to become an important cultural and economic crossroads
and would provide the name for this ocean. Strategically located between
the expanding peoples from the river valley civilizations and insular

Southeast Asia, traders in the Bay of Bengal soon developed what is known as the catamaran. It was not constructed then as the double-hulled vessel that we call by that name today, but as a bundle of logs lashed together to form a sturdy raft. Departing from the Austronesian outrigger canoe, the catamaran indicated an increasing development in shipping technology.

Shipping technology came hand in hand with an increase in trade volume by the beginning of the Common Era. The convenience of the monsoon wind patterns placed increasing demands for new ships to meet the challenges of the open ocean during the stormy seasons. The result was the development of the dhow in the Arabian Sea. This sewn-plank boat came in many varieties, and the largest of them could easily compete with the European ships arriving in the 1500s. Incidentally, it would be these very Europeans who would group all single-hulled ships under the dhow category, regardless of their appearance. The classic feature that these vessels had in common was a triangular lateen sail. Unlike the square sail, which permitted sailing only before the wind, the lateen sail increased the ship's maneuverability against prevailing winds. Hull and sails together provided a perfect craft to withstand the monsoon's might.

Navigating the Indian Ocean was no easy task. It was initially explored in ways similar to those used in the Pacific Islands (see chapter 3). Much of the initial expansion, especially in the western regions of the ocean, was done in close proximity to the shores. Yet as trade routes became longer, open-water mastery became increasingly important. Celestial navigation was key, and it dominated water as well as desert regions. With the expansion of Islam in the 700s, a chain of observatories along coastal regions of the Indian Ocean improved navigational knowledge, and star maps became widely circulated. An instrument known as the astrolabe, probably developed by Greek mariners during the second century BCE, provided help with the determination of latitude by focusing on the Polar (North) Star or the Sun. The magnetic compass from China proved another useful tool, although the rocky nature of the boat ride frequently compromised its helpfulness. Over the years, mariners contributed to the geographical literature and mapmaking of the area and provided the groundwork for future generations.

The first of such geographical texts was the *Periplus of the Erythraean Sea*, written by an anonymous Greek merchant hailing from Egypt in the first century CE. The document describes in great detail the geographical, nautical, and economic conditions of the western shores of the Indian Ocean. The *Periplus* attests to the economic expansion between the Indian

FIGURE 1-2 NAVIGATORS USING AN ASTROLABE
Source: Ms Fr 2810 f.188 Navigators using an astrolabe in the Indian Ocean (vellum), Boucicaut Master (fl.1390-1430) (and workshop)/Bibliotheque Nationale, Paris, France/Bridgeman Art Library.

Ocean and the Mediterranean worlds following the ascension of Roman emperor Augustus (31 BCE–14 CE) that ushered in a period known as Roman peace (*pax Romana*). This era lasted until the end of the 200s and provided a golden age of Greco-Roman commerce in the Indian Ocean. During this time period the Egyptian port of Alexandria grew in importance, and trade from Somalia and the Indian Malabar Coast reached the shores of the Mediterranean Sea. The decline and ultimate fall of the Western Roman Empire prevented further expansion.

RELIGIOUS EXCHANGES IN THE INDIAN OCEAN: BUDDHISM, HINDUISM, JAINISM

During the first centuries of the Common Era, the economic interchange grew increasingly complex, going well beyond foodstuffs and metals. South Asia, which stood at the center of the Indian Ocean trade, supplied aromatics (perfumes), medicines, dyes, and textiles, and also provided a growing market for items from other regions. Southeast Asian producers supplied spices and gemstones and provided an important relaying station for silk and porcelain arriving from China. East Africa grew in importance as a supplier of animal products (especially ivory), gold, and humans (slaves). The Mediterranean waters were more on the receiving end of the exchange, although a minimal trade in wool went to the Indian Ocean. This trade increased after 600 CE.

While the economic impact of early exchanges is difficult to quantify, the cultural impact was significant. In particular, religions and philosophies developed during the period from 600 to about 300 BCE had a substantial impact on peoples on Indian Ocean shores. This is nowhere more apparent than during the so-called Indianization of Southeast Asia, an influence that is reflected in the name Indonesia. Most of these influences derived from South Asian mariners, who integrated existing regional Southeast Asian trade networks into the larger world of the Indian Ocean. At the beginning of the Common Era, Southeast Asian commodities, especially spices, timber, and gemstones, entered the exchange, while Indian cultural influences started to spread to Southeast Asia. Historians are quick to point out, however, that the influences arriving in Southeast Asia were by no means imposed, and local societies were quite selective in their adaptations.

Three major religious influences crossing the Bay of Bengal were Buddhism, Hinduism, and Jainism, the spread of which coincided with the mastery of the Indian Ocean current and wind patterns. These religions emerged out of a dynamic interplay between the established religious manifestations of the Indian subcontinent, referred to as the Vedic tradition (based on a collection of sacred texts known as the Vedas), and a sense of dissatisfaction with its mechanistic rituals. Hinduism, which shared the greatest legacy of the Vedic religions, made the transition from an elite-based faith, with rituals controlled by a selected few, to a vast religion that merged cosmological speculation with local deities. Mythology and an array of stories made this religion popular among the masses. Its ability to blend with local gods and goddesses sat well with Southeast Asian societies.

Jainism originated with Mahavira (~540–468 BCE), who argued, after an extensive period of wandering and meditation, for the existence of a precious life-force animating all living beings. In his effort to preserve this force, Mahavira, who became known as Jina (the conqueror) from which the movement derives its name, established a policy of nonviolence. Jains advocate the preservation of life in all its forms, something that in extreme cases could result in starvation. On the other hand, a Jain lifestyle furthered professions instrumental in the preservation rather than the extinction of life. Jains thus took employment as merchants and bankers, professions vital to the Indian Ocean exchange. Jains became important middlemen in the trade, while introducing their religion to Southeast Asian societies. The stringent lifestyle, however, prevented mass conversion.

Buddhism had a similar origin, but its founder, a prince by the name of Siddhartha Gautama (568–483 BCE) advocated a "middle path" between a life of luxury and one plagued by ascetic withdrawal. Encouraging his followers to realize that all suffering originated in desire, Gauthama urged them to follow a path toward quenching urges and consequently reaching a state of eternal bliss and perpetual tranquility known as Nirvana. Gautama himself was the first to reach this goal, and he became a Buddha (Enlightened One). Traditional Buddhist doctrine focused on the great meditative exertions performed by the individual to reach the state of bliss. Yet in the last century before the Common Era, Buddhism became more popular with the development of the Mahayana variety of this belief system. Mahayana's emphasis on Buddha's compassion, rather than salvation, furthered the concept of bodhisattvas—men and women who stood at the threshold of salvation and opted to forgo their individual enlightenment to guide others on the path. These protectors could be appealed to in time of distress, and by about 200 CE a bodhisattva by the name of Avalokitesvara became the main protector for mariners.

These religions were also portable; that is, they were less associated with sacred geographies and sites, which had dominated the worship of animistic religions in Southeast Asia. While the religions could be practiced anywhere, sites associated with the founders of Buddhism and Jainism grew in popularity and provided an additional export item for Southeast and later East Asia: pilgrims. Travel to significant sites associated with the establishment of these faiths provided an additional incentive for maritime expansion. Pilgrim's attempts to solidify their faith through a visit to a holy site would become even more important with the rise of Islam, in which pilgrimages became institutionalized.

The arrival of new religious configurations in Southeast Asia also had tremendous implications for the area's political development. Traders, mariners, and priests arriving in the region introduced a wealth of ideas. Hindu priests became preferred court advisors, and Indian scripts, especially Sanskrit, became the basis for many written languages in the area. The possibility of linking local kings to reincarnations of Shiva in the Hindu cosmology or a bodhisattva in Mahayana Buddhism provided them with greater political authority. As states started to expand, they frequently employed Indian models of bureaucracy learned through the maritime contact with the South Asian subcontinent. States, which initially drew their strength from controlling local agricultural resources, were now adopting the concept of mandala. This South Asian term refers to courts' use of diplomatic and military resources to gain access to nearby areas. Mandalas were less states in the Western sense than zones of fluctuating powers whose fates waxed and waned according to their influences. Two important states emerging in Southeast Asia following this model were Funan and Srivijaya. Funan, located on the mainland, quickly dominated trade across the Isthmus of Kra, located at the narrowest part of the Malay Peninsula. Merchandise arriving via the Bay of Bengal or the South China Sea was unloaded at this point and quickly carried across by porters. Up to about 500 CE this was a preferred route to avoid the dangerous trip around the Malay Peninsula. Rather than braving pirates and treacherous currents, merchants decided to pay a fee or tax to Funan rulers for food, shelter, and porters.

By 600 CE, a new state appeared on the island of Sumatra. Its name, Srivijaya, was Sanskrit for "Great Conquest." The main "conquest" of this Mandala state was the control over the Strait of Melaka, a narrow, strategic choke point between Sumatra and the Malay Peninsula that allowed for control over the maritime traffic between the Bay of Bengal and the South China Sea. Purging the area temporarily of pirates and other undesirable elements, the rulers of Srivijaya were able to shift the trade center from the Isthmus of Kra to their strategic strait. A powerful navy patrolled the strait and compelled outlying ports to recognize the authority of Srivijaya.

South Asia also felt the impact of new ideas, although from the first millenium CE forward Indian societies there were less inclined to absorb novel cultural influences. Newcomers arriving at the Malabar Coast, across the Arabian Sea, were welcomed but not allowed to integrate into local society. This left arriving foreigners with one important option: limited integration, usually through intermarriage, gave way to what historians call a trade diaspora. In this case, newcomers kept their ethnic and religious identity by exercising control over a significant portion of the maritime trade. The group thus became indispensable for the local community and was therefore not interfered with in any way. Trade diasporas along the South Asian coasts to about 600 CE included Jews and Nestorian Christians. Their belief in one supreme, universal God, who created and sustained the universe, made Jewish individuals a prominent minority throughout the first millennium BCE. The rise of other powerful monotheistic faiths, especially Christianity, brought further complications for Jewish individuals. Christianity, while incorporating the Jewish Scriptures into the Old Testament, also introduced the concept of divine personification through God's son, Jesus Christ. Persecution of Jews increased when Christians blamed them for the death of Christ. As Christianity began spreading throughout the Mediterranean toward the end of the Western Roman Empire, Jewish individuals created trade diasporas, first in Central Asia, and later along the shores of the Indian Ocean where they created settlements as far afield as the Coromandel and the Malabar coasts of the Indian subcontinent. There they were joined by Christians who also experienced persecution. Known as the Nestorians, this particular branch of Christians followed the teachings of the Greek patriarch Nestorius. He argued that while on earth, Jesus ceased his divine form and became a human being. This created a dangerous duality between Christ's human and divine natures and eclipsed Mary's powerful role as the Mother of God. Partially threatened by the Virgin's displacement in Christian theology, Roman Catholic Church officials declared Nestorius's teachings heretical. To avoid further confusion, the Council of Ephesus (431 CE) argued that Christ had two persons (one divine and one human) and allowed the persecution of people who preached otherwise. All but extinguished in the West by the time of the Roman Empire's collapse, the Nestorians too moved on and established important religious trade diasporas along the Indian Ocean, where they operated alongside prominent Jewish communities.

CHINA AND THE INDIAN OCEAN EXCHANGE

Another impulse toward Indian Ocean exchange was the renewed centralization of China under the Tang and Song (618–1279 CE) dynasties. China's vast population had always been a ready market for Indian Ocean merchandise, and Chinese silk and porcelain were prized possessions for foreign merchants. China's extensive coastline and a number of natural harbors suited maritime expansion well, and powerful navies emerged throughout China's rich past.

One of the main factors affecting China's role in the maritime trade network of the Indian Ocean was the attitude of its ruling dynasties. Prior to the Tang and Song dynasties, China's great philosopher, Confucius, greatly influenced China's policies. Historians frequently regard China's Confucian ethics as hostile to maritime exchange. Indeed, Confucius's writings that date to approximately 600 BCE have precious few things to say about this issue. Confucius preferred agriculture over commerce as the state's backbone, and suggested that trade be suppressed lest it interfere with the agricultural output. Yet generally his scorn was aimed at merchants, and less specifically on trade. Trade, Confucius taught, could be a powerful instrument of state expansion, and Chinese dynasties employed it consistently throughout history.

Initially foreign trade relations occurred less along China's shores than along her equally vast land-based frontiers to the north, demarcated by the Great Wall. Following unification under the Qin (221 BCE), strong Chinese dynasties were mirrored by equally strong nomadic confederacies to the north of the Great Wall. There, a number of nomadic peoples developed a powerful cavalry to raid the settled populations of inner China with the aim of extracting resources. Chinese authorities developed a tributary system to deal with the nomadic "problem." While the Chinese dynasties frequently paid tribute to nomadic confederacies, they also employed this strategy to spread their cultural influence beyond the Great Wall of China. Technically this amounted to tribute payments; in reality the tribute included a great deal of trade. The nomads received desired goods from inner China, while the more settled populations received animal products and horses from their nomadic neighbors. This tribute system was later extended to other groups and involved elaborate diplomatic mission meetings with Chinese emperors. When dealing with foreigners not hailing from the nomadic north, the emperors generally demanded acknowledgement of Chinese superiority, a process that was followed by elaborate rituals in later dynasties.

The South China Sea and its connection to the Indian Ocean was initially outside these tribute systems. Following the fall of the Han Dynasty (220 CE), maritime trade was mostly decentralized, falling under the control of local officials loosely attached to a central state authority. With the emergence of the Tang dynasty (618 CE) maritime activities underwent a tremendous growth. Realizing the potential of the Indian Ocean exchange, Tang rulers instituted a Bureau of Maritime Trade run by a commissioner and encouraged trade. The Bureau was responsible for inspecting the arriving commodities and levying import duties. Tang ports experienced a major growth period as authorities provided food, protection, and shelter as major incentives for the settlement of foreigners. During the Tang period, for instance, no less than 4,000 ships visited the port of Guangzhou (Canton) on a yearly basis. As a result, its population became increasingly cosmopolitan. Christians, Jews, Muslims, and Zoroastrians were a frequent sight in and around the port. While foreigners were generally restricted from mingling with the Chinese, Tang authorities tolerated their religions. Following the year 750 CE, Tang authorities became even more dependent on maritime trade as they lost control over the wealthy caravan trade routes in the north. Chinese authorities consequently actively supported their own traders with financial and military resources, enabling them to roam the South China Sea and the Indian Ocean for merchandise. The arrival of precious materials from abroad made those items available beyond the imperial court. Imports included cloves, sandalwood, and tea. Tea drinking, a habit that came to be quintessentially Chinese, also encouraged the development of porcelain production. In time porcelain became a great industry and a valuable export. Besides important trade items, Tang officials actively supported Buddhism, a religion that had reached China in about 400 CE from India. Chinese converts and monks further solidified maritime ties with South Asia as they ventured to visit Buddhist holy sites on their pilgrimages.

But with the increasing arrival of foreigners also came suspicion. Such suspicions were confirmed when a number of Arabs and Persians sacked the city of Guangzhou in 758 after coming in conflict with local Chinese authorities. As Tang rule unraveled, Emperor Wuzong (ruled 840–46) blamed China's problems on foreign influences. He supported indigenous Daoism over foreign Buddhism and Nestorian Christianity, advocating persecutions. Rebellions against the Tang multiplied, and the leader of one of these uprisings sacked Guangzhou a second time in 879, expelling most foreigners. Foreign trade declined for the rest of the Tang Dynasty's rule.

The arrival of the Song Dynasty (960–1279 CE) revived the slumping maritime trade. Keeping many of the Tang institutions geared toward increasing maritime trade, Song rulers added a navy to provide protection for the merchants, especially to shield them from frequent pirate raids This also stimulated the construction of new ships. While the sewn hulls of the dhows could make the trip across the Indian Ocean to the South China Sea, Chinese mariners decided to employ iron-nail-fitted Chinese junks (the anglicized version of the Southeast Asian term *jonk*). The size of these ships continued to increase over the next centuries.

THE EXPANSION OF ISLAM IN THE INDIAN OCEAN

While Chinese action stimulated growth of Indian Ocean trade, it was Islam that served as a lasting unifying cultural force in the area. The rise of Islam was initially peripheral to the Indian Ocean exchange. Yet within a century of this religion's explosion into world history, Muslim merchants not only became active participants in the maritime trade, but became a prominent force. This had much to do with the vital role the religion's teachings allocated to trade. The Prophet Muhammad, who received the recitations later collected in the Qur'an from the Archangel Gabriel, had himself guided caravans from the city of Mecca to Damascus. The holy text makes frequent references to trade, as does a collection of Muhammad's sayings, referred to as the *Hadith*. Two examples illustrate this point: "The honest, truthful Muslim Trader will stand with the martyrs on the Day of Judgment" and "If God permitted the inhabitants of paradise to trade they would deal in cloth and perfume." After establishing a powerbase in Mecca following 630 CE, Muhammad established the five pillars comprising the foundations of the faith. These pillars included the profession of faith, daily prayer, charity, ritual fasting, and an institutionalization of pilgrimage. Pilgrimages were important in the Indian Ocean, but the hajj, as the pilgrimage to Mecca came to be called, institutionalized this practice. Each Muslim was encouraged to visit the Prophet's city at least once during their lifetime. This prescription served as an incentive for maritime trade, and many pilgrims flowed into Jiddah, the port of Mecca located on the Red Sea.

Initial Muslim conquests following Muhammad's death were land-based, wresting important cities from an ailing Sasanid (Persian) Empire. Under the leadership of caliphs (deputies for Muhammad), Muslim forces soon spread into the Middle East and North Africa. A powerful Byzantine (Eastern Roman) Empire arrested much of the Islamic maritime expansion in the Mediterranean and resisted Muslim conquest of Constantinople. A seemingly invincible force on land, Muslims soon created powerful citadels from which they controlled conquered territories. On many occasions, the conquerors allowed Christian and Jewish communities to continue their religious worship. However, a tax was levied for this freedom of worship, something that served also as an informal incentive for conversion. As much as the expanding Islamic forces were successful in winning new converts for their faith, they were converted to the splendor and relative wealth of urban centers. Initial citadels became important cities themselves and key avenues for expansion into the Indian Ocean. The most important of these were Basra and Cairo.

As the expanding Muslim forces sought to consolidate the conquered land, they developed dynasties. The first of these, the Umayyad (661–750 CE) operated out of the important city of Damascus. When Umayyad rulers were replaced by the vibrant Abbasid dynasty (750–1236 CE), a shift in capital cities occurred. Baghdad replaced Damascus, and Basra became a major port on the Persian Gulf. The importance of the Red Sea declined, best seen in the rapid decay of the port of Alexandria, and the gulf now figured as an important avenue for trade. Muslim merchants, encouraged by the words of the Prophet Muhammad, embarked on their mercantile conquest. They followed the Islamic conquest of the Indian province of Sind (710 CE). This province, with its neighbor Gujarat, had been instrumental in supplying merchants and mariners for the pre-Islamic trade in the Indian Ocean. Now, with some of the most important ports in Muslim hands, traders hailing from the Arabian Peninsula entered existing exchange lanes in the Indian Ocean and appeared off the coasts of Southeast and East Asia.

Guided by the example of Muhammad, who was a merchant as well as a prophet, merchants found no major contradictions between trade and proselytizing, and quickly combined roles. It is in the context of the Indian Ocean that the term "jihad" disassociates itself from the common mistranslation of "Holy War." Better translated as "an effort or a striving," jihad can come in four forms: by the heart (referring to the internal struggle to serve Allah), by the sword (referring to the overstressed meaning of the term), by the tongue, and by the hand. The last two varieties refer to the struggle of spreading the religion through words and deeds, both well within the merchant's expertise. Frequently recorded observations of arriving Muslim vessels speak of religious individuals who accompanied merchants on their journey. These individuals usually hailed from the Sufi order, composed of individuals who eschewed the dry legal texts of the Muslim scholars to search for a mystic experience of Allah. While serving as spiritual guides for merchants and sailors during the seascape voyages, Sufis took on the role of missionaries when arriving in ports. At the beginning of the second millennium CE, Islam became very much a cosmopolitan belief system with an international flavor. This allowed people who dwelled on the coast to connect themselves to the emerging Muslim culture across the Indian Ocean, while at the same time distancing themselves from what they regarded as backward local religious expressions of their inland peoples. What was occurring around 1000 CE in the Indian Ocean was something that would later occur in other oceans as well: individuals felt more affinity with the port cultures emerging along the rim of the ocean than with the people living in the immediate hinterland of the port. An international maritime culture was developing, and its cultural glue was provided by the Islamic faith.

ISLAM AND EAST AFRICA

The development of such cultural linkages is best exemplified by the spread of Islam into East Africa and Southeast Asia following the year 1100. Ever since the growth of Indian Ocean trade, East Africa had an important role in the exchange. In antiquity, the Egyptians had established a lively trade with the inhabitants of the Somali Coast. The *Periplus,* that first-century description of the western Indian Ocean, describes several important places along the East African coast that were key for traders coming from the Arabian Peninsula and India's western shores. Such trade increased over the next few centuries. Much of the East African trade was with the province of Gujarat on the western coast of India. Increases in rice agriculture in India had reached a peak, which freed workers for an emerging garment industry. Cotton garments became a major export item that found ready takers in East Africa in return for animal products, gold, and slaves.

Merchants and mariners arriving in East Africa from Gujarat found a maritime environment similar to their own, which included lagoons, tidal flats, and river estuaries. Changing monsoon wind patterns helped increase trade, but also provided for long periods of residence while waiting for a shift in winds. This residency fostered increasing links with the indigenous population, some cemented through gift exchange relationships, some through kin relations. During the first millennium CE, a distinctive culture and society emerged, stretching from the Horn of Africa down to Mozambique. The culture was generally African, but borrowed fundamental aspects from the foreign elements. The most important of these was Islam. As Muslim merchants arrived in ever greater numbers, they began to control not only the more global Indian Ocean trade but also regional exchange patterns. While competing urban centers emerged along the East African coast, the increasing Muslim population demanded conversion of local rulers. They did not have to resort to brute force, threatening instead to move on to the next city, should the rulers not embrace their religion. Intrigued by the cosmopolitan nature of Islam, which provided a clear distinction from the spiritual beliefs of the inland area population, local rulers quickly realized that the establishment of mosques and other facilities dedicated to Islam provided an additional incentive for merchant settlement.

In addition to a fluid culture, which combined Muslim with indigenous African values, a distinctive trade language started to develop: Swahili. Deriving from the Arabic term for coast, Swahili is essentially a Bantu (African) language with a number of Arabic and Persian, and later Portuguese, terms woven into it. The influence of Islam and the Qur'an also introduced Arabic script, which was used to record developments along the Swahili coast. Cities emerging along the coast evolved into important trade emporia that frequently competed with each other. Archaeological excavations in East Africa have revealed merchandise from all major focal points of the Indian Ocean. While no single urban center was able to dominate the entire trade along the coast, there seems to be ample evidence that individual cities exercised considerable control over the area. The city of Kilwa (located on an offshore island in contemporary Tanzania), with its gold and slave trades, dominated this portion of the Indian Ocean trade from 1250 to 1350 before economic hegemony moved to the port city of Mombasa (in contemporary Kenya). By the 1500s, the Portuguese joined in the Swahili coast exchange and eclipsed the power of many local coastal cities.

The impact of the Swahili city-states on the African continent is clearly uneven. While some societies were hardly impacted, frequent contact with the Swahili coast led to the establishment of Great Zimbabwe. Bantu-speaking Shona peoples established a thriving settlement in the vicinity of the Zambezi river that probably served as an important trade connection between the Swahili coast and the peoples residing in Africa's center. By 1400, the inhabitants of Great Zimbabwe had developed into skilled miners who contributed gold and copper ornaments to the trade, receiving in return important cotton garments and porcelain from India and China.

ISLAM AND SOUTHEAST ASIA

Another area that felt the impact of Muslim traders was Southeast Asia. There, arriving Muslim merchants met with a number of well-established cosmopolitan faiths, such as Buddhism and Hinduism, which had already crossed the watery expanse from South Asia. Focus turned to the city of Melaka, which arose as an important trade emporium located along the strait of the same name. When the Sumatran Prince Paramesvara established the city in the early 1400s, he quickly realized that ample water supply and a relatively mild climate would attract many merchants. The mangrove-free harbor was large enough to accommodate even the largest ships during this time period. The city also competed with many established states in the region; the largest of these was the Buddhist Thai Kingdom to the north of Melaka. To ensure protection, Paramesvara and his successors sent diplomatic missions to Ming China and became part of their elaborate tribute system. Some accounts show Paramesvara visiting China three times on tribute missions. Another factor in Melaka's success was that its rulers embraced Islam as their religion, whereupon many Muslim merchants made Melaka their preferred port of call. The arrival of this new religion came in the form of a marriage alliance between the ruler of Melaka and those residing in the port of Pasai on Sumatra. The nominal alliance with China and the financial support of Muslim merchants made Melaka one of the most powerful emporia in the Indian Ocean. Unlike many other coastal cities in Southeast Asia, Melaka did not have a rich agricultural hinterland to stimulate the growth of the urban center. Melaka was thus entirely dependent on the maritime trade of the Indian Ocean. To manage the traffic flowing through this bustling city, the rulers employed four harbor masters, each of them dealing with a particular region of the Indian Ocean. Paramesvara's successors also ordered the construction of vast underground storage facilities, which protected valued merchandise against the elements of the ocean (floods) and human failure or sabotage (fire), thus providing an additional stimulus for merchants arriving in the city. Early European visitors to the region reported almost 70 languages spoken in the city's streets. Not only did Melaka benefit from increased commercial standing after conversion to Islam, but Muslims now used Melaka as a springboard to spread into insular and mainland Southeast Asia. The country known as Indonesia today is the most populated Muslim country in the world, even if it is farthest removed from the religion's point of origin. It was from Melaka that Islam spread to the Malay Peninsula and increased the number of converts throughout the islands of Java and Sumatra. By the end of the 1400s, Melaka's patronage of the Islamic faith provided an extension of Muslim conversion into the Philippine archipelago, where it would soon compete with another universalizing religion: Christianity (see chapter 3).

As Islam expanded into insular Southeast Asia, it underwent transformations. Although there are precious few documents about the initial arrival of Islam in the region, many believe that Islamic traders and accompanying Sufi mystics planted the religion's first seeds. Especially on the island of Java, the more mystical teachings of the Sufis merged with local religious practice. In a process known as syncretism (a process that defines the joining together of two different cultural practices to create novel institutions while retaining some of the earlier traditions), the Javanese variety of Islam remained devoutly monotheistic. At the same time, however, Javanese frequently emphasized the divine nature of human beings. This practice spoke to existing religious traditions predating the arrival of Islam.

COSMOPOLITAN TRAVELERS AND THE INDIAN OCEAN

Despite intermittent conflict in the Indian Ocean region, the area became increasingly cosmopolitan. This is best illustrated by two well-documented accounts of travelers who ventured to the region: Marco Polo and Ibn Battuta. Their accounts provide a vivid picture of the Indian Ocean and regions of Central and East Asia in the latter half of the 1200s and the first half of the

1300s. Their accounts are similar in that neither one of them committed his story to paper, receiving instead assistance from others. Because they were assisted by a romance writer and an Islamic scholar respectively, their works shared a wide readership in the Christian and Islamic world. Similarly, the presence of tall stories led to increasing criticism throughout the last centuries. Scholars frequently question whether or not Ibn Battuta and Polo visited all the regions they describe in their narratives. There is at least one historian who argues that Polo derived his accounts from the stories of other merchants, while never venturing much beyond the Black Sea.

Moving beyond the similarities, Polo's and Ibn Battuta's accounts differ greatly, a fact that also speaks to their subsequent impact. Ibn Battuta's narrative is written in the form of a *rihla*, a literary genre that centers on a journey or pilgrimage to Mecca, the holiest of Islamic cities. Although Ibn Battuta was a frequent visitor to Mecca, his journeys of close to 70,000 miles (undertaken between 1325 and 1355) took him from his native Tangiers in North Africa to the most distant corners of Dar-al-Islam (the abode of Islam, or the Islamic world). Ibn Battuta, while frequently venturing into unfamiliar territory, journeyed a world that shared the Islamic faith as a unifying feature. A Sufi scholar himself, Ibn Battuta found shelter among fellow mystical individuals who helped him understand the commonalities and differences of the Dar-al-Islam. His accounts thus celebrate the cosmopolitanism of the Islamic world, spanning the length of the Indian Ocean world. Not a keen sailor, Ibn Battuta spent little time dwelling on nautical knowledge or maritime technology. As far as the Indian Ocean world is concerned, however, Ibn Battuta's *rihla* underscores the reach of Islam and the commonalities of prominent port towns in East Africa, India, and Southeast Asia. When Iba Battuta returned from his journeys, he enlisted the help of a young Islamic scholar to put it on paper. The resulting *rihla* greatly celebrated the Islamic societies spanning the Indian Ocean, assuring his narrative a prominent status among Muslims over the next 600 years.

Marco Polo's account could scarcely be more contrasting. The Venetian's work is essentially divided into two major parts. The first one of these summarizes his journey to East Asia, while the second one speaks in a didactic manner about the marvels and information that he gathered while traveling (1271–95) east to China. Unlike Ibn Battuta, Polo traveled accompanied by his father and uncle in what was largely unfamiliar territory to Europeans. Mongol expansion, following the rise of its universal ruler (better known as Genghis Khan) had unified much of Central Asia and provided a short-lived unity to the overland exchange routes, known collectively as the Silk Routes. While Polo met fellow Europeans along his journey, they figured as notable exceptions to the many "odd" practices he encountered. Once he arrived in Mongol-controlled China he encountered emperor Kublai Khan. The founder of the Yuan dynasty was greatly taken by the young Polo and offered him a job as a foreign advisor. Polo returned to his native Venice, leaving China on a sea voyage through the Indian Ocean, allowing him to comment broadly on the area. Shortly after his return, Polo served on a Venetian vessel that was promptly captured by the Genoese. Awaiting his fate in prison, Polo told his story to a romance writer, who committed it on paper. It is unclear whether Polo exaggerated the account, but tall stories underlying his report made him suspect even among contemporaries. His story was written from a merchant's perspective and spoke widely about the riches in precious stones, textiles, and spices found along the overland routes in Central Asia and the maritime exchange lanes of the Indian Ocean. Writing about the island of Sumatra, Polo commented:

> It contains an abundance of riches and all sorts of spices, aloes woods, sapanwood for dyeing, and various other kinds of drugs, which on account of the length of the voyage and the danger ... are not only imported into our country, but which find their way to the [Chinese] provinces.

Polo's account talks about a strange world lying beyond the known confines of the European world, yet, unlike Ibn Battuta's writing, Polo's has little celebration of the societies encountered. Furthermore, Polo's *Voyage* lacks the cosmopolitan self-reflective qualities of Ibn Battuta's *rihla*. But therein lays the appeal of Polo's narrative. Extolling the economic wealth and potential of the regions he traveled, Polo's *Voyage* served as an inspiration to fellow European explorers and travelers. It is certain that Polo's account contributed in no small measure to the European expansions that followed. Christopher Columbus, for instance, not only used Polo's narrative to plan his westerly voyage through the Atlantic Ocean, but also took a copy with him on his ship. Where Ibn Battuta's report gained its currency from a reflexive celebratory description of the Islamic world, Polo's tale encouraged further exploration and expansion. Polo's *Voyage* thus stands as a prelude to the European expansion into the Indian Ocean that followed roughly two hundred years after his narrative was published.

CHINESE AND IBERIAN VENTURES IN THE INDIAN OCEAN

The 1400s witnessed the arrival of two major powers in the Indian Ocean—China and Portugal. Both were attracted to the wealth of the Indian Ocean, but their impacts on the region were quite different. Chinese ventures to the region were short-lived, while the Portuguese initiated an extended period of European incursion into the Indian Ocean. Chinese interest in the Indian Ocean continued unabated even after the Mongol conquest in 1279. The newly established Mongol Yuan dynasty, under Kublai Khan, continued the active promotion of maritime trade begun by Tang and Song rulers. The main difference was that the Yuan dynasty generally preferred the patronage of foreign merchants (especially Arabs and Indians) over indigenous Chinese traders. The Mongols also extended their influence into Burma, Vietnam, and Korea; however, two large-scale military invasions of the islands of Japan attempted in the 1200s ended in dismal failure.

Later, when the indigenous Han Chinese rose against the Mongols in the 1300s, the newly formed Ming dynasty (1368–1644) sought to expand Chinese presence in the Indian Ocean. This was especially true of the Yongle emperor (r. 1403–24), who ordered the refurbishing and expansion of the existing navy in an attempt to return Chinese greatness to the Indian Ocean. The main purpose of the expansion was to convince peoples around the Indian Ocean of the commercial and political might of the Ming dynasty. As such, the Yongle emperor hoped to integrate the contacted societies in a restored and expanded tributary system. A total of seven expeditions sailed from China between 1405 and 1433, eclipsing by far prior maritime endeavors. In fact, it was not until the First World War that the Ming endeavors would finally be surpassed. The leader of the Yongle expedition was the eunuch admiral Zheng He. Zheng He was born into a Muslim family of Mongol descent. When expanding Ming troops reached his province, he was captured and served as a palace slave. His affiliation with the Yongle emperor enabled him to rise through the ranks and earn him an appointment as admiral of the Ming fleet. His Muslim faith and upbringing proved to be an important factor in this appointment. The Yongle emperor hoped Zheng He's background would appeal to the many Islamic societies residing along the shores of the Indian Ocean.

The first expedition in 1405 was also the largest, numbering close to 300 ships, including some so-called "treasure ships." These nine-masted giants measured a good 300 feet in length and 150 feet in width and had a carrying capacity of almost 3,000 tons. Almost 27,000 soldiers sailed with this armada, in addition to translators and diplomats. The first three expeditions went to the South China Sea and the Bay of Bengal, with the fourth venturing to the Arabian Sea and the Persian Gulf. Subsequent expeditions went to the Red Sea and down the Swahili Coast. Loaded with treasured Chinese silk and porcelain, Zheng He showered his hosts with gifts and returned with exotic animals (such as giraffes) and scores of emissaries willing to pay their respect to the Ming rulers. Zheng He campaigned against pirates in the South China Sea and paid respect to local rulers. Following the death of the Yongle emperor in 1424, however, Ming support for the expeditions started to wane. Ministers who mistrusted Zheng He's Muslim background deemed the expeditions too costly and preferred to shift their resources toward warding off a mounting Mongol threat in northwest China. At the conclusion of the seventh expedition, funding for the expansion disappeared, nautical charts and records about the Indian Ocean were destroyed, and the treasure fleet was left to rot in the harbors. While China's political might in the Indian Ocean was fleeting, Chinese merchants continued to ride the tide of Zheng He's expansion. These merchants established a prominent trade diaspora that proved beneficial to both local rulers and Europeans arriving in the Indian Ocean at the end of the 1400s.

European connection to the Indian Ocean necessitates recapitulation. Preceding pages spoke of a long-standing connection of the Mediterranean world to the Indian Ocean dating back to the first millennium before the birth of Christ. The disintegration of the Roman Empire and the expansion of Islam made this connection difficult but did not sever it. Marco Polo's own travel account attests to the rising might of Italian trade cities that dominated the eastern Mediterranean following the year 1100. Polo's presence in China represented just a distant branch of a strong Genoese and Venetian influence that was based on several circumstances. The first of these was a set of holy campaigns fought by Christian states against the Islamic occupation of the sacred sites around the city of Jerusalem. These campaigns are collectively known as the Crusades (1095–1291). Following the conquest of Jerusalem (1099), an emerging number of crusader states enabled Italian merchants to secure favored-nation status on the emerging trade. The second aspect of rising Genoese and Venetian trade was an emerging conflict among crusaders and the Byzantine Empire that encouraged Italian takeover of strategic islands (such as Crete) in the eastern Mediterranean. Genoese and Venetian imports of slaves, spices, sugar, and textiles whetted Europeans' appetite for these products. The expulsion of the Crusaders from the Holy Land in 1291 as well as the loss of Mongol control over the overland exchanges in 1350 encouraged especially the Genoese to explore trading possibilities in the western Mediterranean Sea. Fortunately for the Genoese traders, Christian forces had commenced a sustained campaign to expel Muslim forces from Spain and had opened the Strait of Gibraltar (between the Iberian Peninsula and North Africa) for merchants.

Marco Polo's account well illustrated the rising interests of Italian merchants in the Indian Ocean. Another prominent source was the Catalan atlas now housed in the Biblioteque National in Paris. This document was most likely crafted by Abraham Cresques in 1375. Cresques was a Catalonian Jew who hailed from the island of Majorca, with close connections to the Spanish ruling houses. This connection enabled Cresques to access most of the information available in Catalonia in his crafting of the map. Much like Polo's narrative, the Catalan atlas merges facts and mythological tales. Yet it also depicts the wealth of the Indian Ocean region. On the atlas, colorful islands with wealthy rulers are surrounded by an ocean with floating spices. Cresques's creation shows how the well-explored Mediterranean world opens up to regions whose economic potential is apparent, but the extent of which remains unexplored. Polo's written account and Cresques's visual document serve as important points of departure for the Iberian expansion.

The Mediterranean frontier also encouraged Portuguese expansion in the 1400s. The loss of Constantinople to Ottoman (Turk) forces in 1453 provided an additional incentive to sail to the slave- and gold-rich shores of Africa. By 1488, Bartholomeu Dias rounded the tip of Africa and stood on the threshold of the Indian Ocean. His journey was cut short, however, by powerful storms and threat of mutiny. Less than 10 years later, Vasco da Gama rounded the Cape of Good Hope and arrived in the Indian Ocean. His fleet was a far cry from that of Zheng He, whose largest vessel was six times the size of Vasco da Gama's, and his four ships would have been no match for the Ming dynasty's exploration armadas. Da Gama's strategies differed greatly from those of the Chinese admiral. While Zheng He used violence only when confronted with pirates and noncooperative hosts, da Gama's encounters were frequently marred by violence. Da Gama quickly realized that his coarse and entirely inappropriate textiles, when compared to Chinese silks, generated little interest, so he resorted to blunt force for trade. His brief stays in Mozambique and Mombassa ended in gun battles, and he took emissaries hostage in Malindi until he received a pilot to guide him to India. Arriving in Calicut on the Malabar Coast, da Gama again realized that he had very little of interest to offer. He stayed three months, stretching the host's welcome, and returned to Europe with a small but priceless cargo of spices. Not only did these spices pay for the entire expedition, but they incited the Portuguese to send further and larger expeditions that built on the path of destruction laid out by da Gama. Over the next years powerful Portuguese fleets arrived in the Indian Ocean. Numbering almost 80 ships, they accounted for a combined firepower of 7,000 men. While this was still short of Zheng He's fabled treasure fleets, the Portuguese were not reluctant to use their might. Their tactics proved successful: launch quick strikes against strategic choke

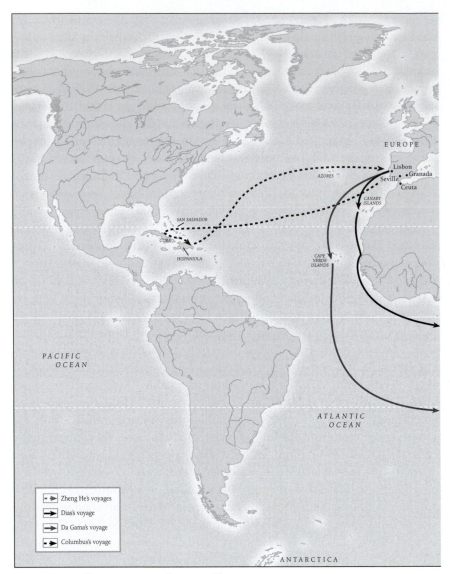

FIGURE 1-3 IBERIAN AND CHINESE EXPANSIONS
Source: Used with permission from Traditions and Encounters (2nd ed.), by Jerry H. Bentley and Herbert F. Ziegler. Copyright 2002 by McGraw-Hill.

points along the Indian Ocean and proceed to fortify them. By 1505, they had established a significant presence along the Swahili coast. They occupied Goa along the Malabar Coast in 1510; Hormuz, an important point at the entrance of the Persian Gulf, fell in 1508; and by 1511 they had con-

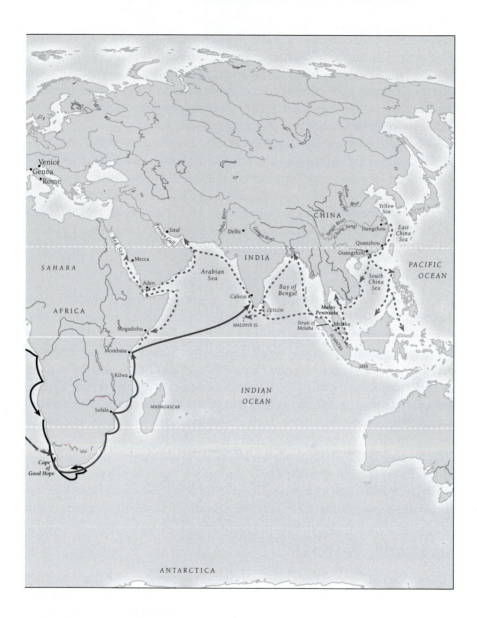

quered Melaka and were now controlling significant trade between the Pacific and Indian oceans. By 1557, the Portuguese established a presence in Macao, an island off the China coast.

Reaction to the Portuguese encroachment varied. Some powerful empires, such as the Mughals of India, tolerated the Portuguese presence. They left the control over the maritime lanes to the Portuguese and preferred to oversee terrestrial control over India. The Ottoman Turks objected greatly to the Portuguese and joined alliances with the Egyptian and Gujarati forces. The Portuguese victory over this alliance in the Battle of Diu (1509) proved that the Ottoman galleys were no match for faster and more maneuverable Iberian vessels. The Ottoman sultan ultimately relented and focused his conquests on terrestrial domains of eastern Europe.

By 1515 the Portuguese assumed at least a nominal control over the Indian Ocean. Taking out the Muslim middlemen in the spice trade, they broke the back of Genoese and Venetian commerce. Their *Estado do India* (Portuguese Empire) was a rather porous affair, as the Portuguese had fewer than 10,000 armed men stationed in the whole of the Indian Ocean. Yet their ruthless tactics had consolidated a considerable amount of trade in their hands.

CONCLUSION

The overall development of an Indian Ocean world was a gradual affair that took the better part of two millennia. The decoding of the important monsoon regime governing the winds in the area was one challenge to overcome; constructing powerful vessels that could resist the constant beatings of the waters and the elements was another. Once these goals were accomplished, a lively exchange occurred by the first century CE that brought together peoples from Africa to China. Besides trade of significant goods that included staples as well as luxury items, there was also an exchange in religion, involving in particular Buddhism, Hinduism, and Islam. It was Islam that dominated Indian Ocean exchanges until the arrival of the Europeans in the late 1400s. European expansion into the Indian Ocean formed part of a larger exploratory pattern that would take Spanish and Portuguese mariners into first the Atlantic and later the Pacific oceans.

SUGGESTED READINGS

The number of general texts on the Indian Ocean is growing continuously. Some of the most significant volumes are Kenneth McPherson's *The Indian Ocean: A History of People and the Sea* (Oxford: Oxford University Press, 1998) and more recently, *The Indian Ocean* by Michael Pearson (New York: Routledge, 2003). Milo Kearney's *The Indian Ocean in World History* (New York: Routledge, 2004) attempts to map the Indian Ocean within the framework of accepted civilizations and empires. For an economic history of the Indian Ocean, consult, K. N. Chaudhuri's *Trade and Civilization in the Indian Ocean: An Economic History from the Rise of Islam to 1750* (New York:

Cambridge University Press, 1985) and his *Asia before Europe: Economy and Civilization of the Indian Ocean from the Rise of Islam to 1750* (New York: Cambridge University Press, 1990). For an interesting exploration of archaeological research on early Indian Ocean travel and religious exchange, see Himanshu Prabah Ray's *The Winds of Change: Buddhism and the Maritime Links of Early South Asia* (New York: Oxford University Press, 1998) and her *The Archaeology of Seafaring in Ancient South Asia* (New York: Cambridge University Press, 2003). On a historical exploration of early East African contribution to the Indian Ocean, see Christopher Ehret's *An African Classical Age: Eastern and Southern Africa in World History, 1000 B.C. to A.D. 400* (Charlottsville: University of Virgina Press, 1998). L. Casson edited the classical document delineating trade routes in the western Indian Ocean during the first century: *The Periplus Maris Erythraei* (Princeton: Princeton University Press, 1989). A number of accounts deal with the Indian Ocean during Islamic times. About the Swahili Coast, see Michael N. Pearson's *Port Cities and Intruders: The Swahili Coast, India, and Portugal in the Early Modern Era* (Baltimore: Johns Hopkins University Press, 1998). On development of seafaring during the Islamic times, consult George F. Hourani, *Arab Seafaring in the Indian Ocean in Ancient and Medieval Times*, rev. ed. (Princeton: Princeton University Press, 1995). On the development of trade during Islamic times, see Patricia Risso's *Merchants and Faith: Muslim Commerce and Culture in the Indian Ocean* (Boulder: Westview Press, 1995). Regarding the development of the Indian Ocean trade along Chinese coasts, consult Gang Deng, *Chinese Maritime Activities and Socioeconomic Development, c. 2100 B.C.–1900 A.D.* (Westport, CT: Greenwood Press, 1997), and his *Maritime Sector, Institutions, and Sea Power of Premodern China* (Westport, CT: Greenwood Press, 1999). About the voyages of the Ming Dynasty, explore Louise Levathes's *When China Ruled the Seas: The Treasure Fleet of the Dragon Throne* (New York: Oxford University Press, 1996). For an intriguing account of the Indian Ocean's role in pre-European economic systems, consult Janet Abu-Lughod, *Before European Hegemony: The World System A.D. 1250–1350* (New York: Oxford University Press, 1989), especially chapters 6–10. For a classical account of the Portuguese expansion into the Indian Ocean, see Charles Boxer's *The Portuguese Seaborn Empire, 1415-1825* (New York: Alfred Knopf, 1969). A more recent work is Sanjay Subrahmanyam's *The Portuguese Empire in Asia, 1500-1700: A Political and Economic History* (London: Longman, 1993). A nice contrast between Marco Polo and Ibn Battuta can be found in Ross E. Dunn, *The Adventures of Ibn Battuta: A Muslim Traveler of the 14th Century* (Los Angeles: University of California Press, 1986), especially introduction and chapter 14.

CHAPTER TWO TIMELINE

500 BCE	Arawaks reach the Caribbean Islands
1000 CE	Viking voyages to North America
1300	Muslim traders link Mediterranean with Saharan Atlantic
1420–60	Strong encouragement for Portuguese voyages
1444	First documented import of African slaves to Europe
1488	Bartholomeu Dias sails around the Cape of Good Hope
1492	Christopher Columbus reaches Americas
1494	Treaty of Tordesillas settles Portuguese and Spanish disputes; it is ignored by most other European nations
1520–40	Principal decades of Spanish conquest in the Americas
1500–1650	"Colombian Exchanges" impact societies on both sides of the Atlantic
1775	Beginning of the American Revolution
1789	Beginning of the French revolution
1791	Beginning of the Haitian Revolution
1810–24	Revolutions in the Americas

CHAPTER TWO

CULTURAL AND BIOLOGICAL EXCHANGES IN THE ATLANTIC OCEAN

GETTING STARTED ON CHAPTER TWO: What types of currents determined the exploration of the Atlantic Ocean? What type of exchanges governed the Atlantic Ocean world? What were the roles of Africans, Europeans, and Native Americans in the area? What type of revolutions changed and molded the Atlantic region?

CHAPTER OUTLINE

Introduction

The Complexities of Navigation: Mastering Atlantic Winds and Currents

Columbian Exchanges

   Diseases

   Power

   Animals and Plants

African Migrations to the Americas

Transatlantic Revolutions

   North America

   France and Haiti

   South America

Conclusion

INTRODUCTION

Compared to the Indian Ocean, whose historic integration started some 4,000 years ago, the Atlantic has a rather shallow timeframe within human history. Historians even possess an exact date for the beginnings of Atlantic integration: 1492, or Christopher Columbus's first trip across this ocean. It is Columbus's voyages and those following in his wake that frequently lead scholars to the assumption that the Atlantic is in fact a European "artifact." While there is some truth to this assertion, since following the 1500s Europeans did successfully negotiate the current and wind regimes of the Atlantic Ocean, other peoples contributed to this process as well. The Americas were not just empty continents upon European arrival, although diseases and conquest soon decimated Amerindian populations. Likewise, the shipping of Africans in bondage across the Atlantic was the result of complex negotiations occurring along African shores. Enslaved Africans in no small measure contributed to the cultural and demographic development of the Americas and the making of the Atlantic world.

This chapter charts the slow but steady understanding of winds and currents dominating the Atlantic Ocean. Then, without spending too much time on Columbus's well-known story, the chapter investigates the exchanges named after him: a complex set of relations involving animals, diseases, peoples, and plants. The remainder of the chapter delineates the societies in Africa and the Americas that emerged as a consequence of the "Columbian Exchanges." It concludes with an exploration of revolutionary activity along the Atlantic Rim.

THE COMPLEXITIES OF NAVIGATION: MASTERING ATLANTIC WINDS AND CURRENTS

The Atlantic Ocean is the second largest of the earth's oceans and currently the most heavily traveled. Although the Atlantic, like the Indian Ocean, has fuzzy boundaries, the ocean proper has a surface area of about 31,660,000 square miles (about 82 million square kilometers). Bordering the ocean are the four continents of Africa, Europe, and North and South America, all of whose peoples played a pivotal role in making an integrated Atlantic world.

The ocean's name finds its origin in Greek mythology. According to a frequently told story, Atlas and his brother Hesperus once stood at the ocean's shore. To gain a better perspective Hesperus climbed on Atlas's shoulder. Once he had reached the giant's shoulder, Hesperus was unable to hold on and fell headlong into the ocean, but not before tearing out a piece of Atlas's flesh. According to the tale, the chunk of flesh became the mythical place known as Atlantis, and the surrounding waters became known as the Atlantic. Ultimately, Atlas's journeys came to an end when he supported the titans in their struggle against the Greek gods. For this misdeed, Zeus condemned Atlas to bear the heavens on his shoulder.

In all its splendor, the Atlantic proved to be a difficult adversary to human settlement and had for millennia separated the peoples of the Americas from those of Afro-Eurasia. While parts of the Atlantic Ocean were well known to Mediterranean, African, and Native American societies, wind directions and ocean currents presented formidable obstacles. From a European perspective, for instance, dominant winds in the northern hemisphere, blowing in the north-eastern direction, prevented easy western expansion. European mariners had to head north toward Norway in order to reach the favorable eastern Greenland current that facilitated westward sailing. It is thus not surprising that the Vikings became the first sailors to brave these routes. Catching available currents from Scandinavia, the Vikings settled Greenland probably before 1000 CE. Using the world's largest island as a springboard, the Norsemen sailed on the Labrador current all the way to Newfoundland (a large island off the coast of Canada). Archaeological evidence confirms the Norse Sagas, as Viking settlements have been uncovered in L'Anse aux Meadows (Newfoundland). The settlement was brief, however, as arduous supply routes and violent encounters with native peoples soon forced the sites' abandonment.

The Vikings were not the only ones exploring current and wind directions in the Atlantic Ocean. Ultimately it would be sailors emerging from the Mediterranean Sea who established a long-lasting presence. Long before the Vikings, the Phoenicians had encountered the so-called Canary current (after the islands of the same name) that made voyages from the Mediterranean to West Africa possible, but at the same time prevented return travel. Following in their footsteps were Arab merchants who ventured down the coast of West Africa only to return to the Mediterranean Sea via the Saharan overland routes. For Muslims, the Atlantic encouraged important psychological boundaries. The frequently tempestuous ocean with its towering waves acquired the name *al-bahr-al-Maghim* (the Sea of Perpetual Gloom). Nevertheless, Muslim merchants did reach the port of Salé, about 300 kilometers from Gibraltar in the south of the Iberian Peninsula. Such maritime expansion frequently linked with trans-Saharan overland caravans going as far afield as the rivers Niger and Senegal.

It was through these very trade routes that the Mediterranean world was in contact with the emerging Islamic kingdoms in West Africa. Two quite different "seas" characterized these worlds. The climate of the Mediterranean Sea dictated the world of the various peoples living along her shores. Conversely, the Sahara desert influenced the West African world. The Sahara is not a sea in the strict sense of the word, but with its shifting sands and lack of potable water, it is equally difficult to navigate. The domestication and later introduction of the camel, sometimes referred to as the "desert's flagship," by about 500 BCE provided nomads living on the edge of this arid region the opportunity to explore its boundaries. Mapping oases along the way, they established important trade routes that would bring slaves and gold from West Africa to Mediterranean shores. The introduction of Islam following the 600s also affected the nomads, who, among others, were instrumental in spreading the religion to West Africa.

In essence, the Mediterranean and the Saharan Atlantic were finally linked following the 1300s. There was much interest in the Mediterranean to reach West Africa for its ample supply of gold and slaves, and the sea route had distinct advantages over the caravan route through the Saharan desert. First, sea trade would open quicker and safer routes than those crossing the arid desert. Second, the ships' greater cargo holds could quickly outcompete the intermediaries controlling trade in the Sahara. Yet the Canary current frustrated the return voyage and put daring merchants in danger. The Vivaldi brothers, for instance, departed Genoa in 1291 to set sail for the riches of West Africa and to reach the spice-rich Indian Ocean. They were never heard from again. Cape Bojador, located on the edge of Morocco and the onset of the Canary current, became the point of no return for most controlled voyages.

European and Arab mariners were not the only ones interested in Atlantic expansion. For their part, African navigators were just as interested in reaching the trade-rich Mediterranean Basin, of which they had extensive knowledge through the Saharan trade routes. But going there proved difficult. The same Canary current that allowed uncontrolled Mediterranean expansion to West Africa prevented those inhabitants from sailing north. Currents and winds could have taken Africans to the Caribbean Basin, but their commerce had long been oriented around the desert trade routes, and they consequently declined to investigate nautical technology. Inhabitants of the West African shores nevertheless developed extensive trade connections between the rivers Senegal and Gambia, frequently using these rivers to contact peoples living upstream.

On the other side of the Atlantic, the indigenous peoples of the Caribbean developed a thriving maritime culture. The evidence is, unfortunately, sketchy and based almost exclusively on early Spanish accounts.

Yet it seems that besides dugout canoes, the peoples of Mesoamerica and the Caribbean developed double-hulled canoes and the necessary sails to propel them. Whether these items were used in the original settlement of the Caribbean islands is uncertain. Archaeological and ethnohistorical knowledge suggests, however, that Caribbean peoples employed such canoes for the purposes of trade and warfare. Currently available evidence is insufficient to support Amerindian transatlantic travel, especially since the very currents that could have taken the Africans to the Caribbean Basin worked against the inhabitants of these regions.

The move to bring these different worlds together came from the people inhabiting the Mediterranean Atlantic. Mastering the open Atlantic Ocean required both knowledge of currents and wind and changes in ship construction. While societies around the Mediterranean Sea had developed a number of ships since antiquity, their constructions, usually involving oars as well as square sails, were ill-equipped for the violent nature of the Atlantic Ocean. A revolution in shipbuilding came from the marriage of Mediterranean nautical technology with that available in the Atlantic's

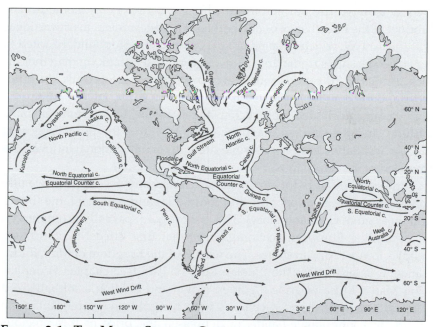

FIGURE 2-1 THE MAJOR SURFACE CURRENTS OF THE OCEANS

Source: Used with permission from An Introduction to the World's Oceans (8th ed.), *by Keith Sverdrup, Alyn C. Duxbury, and Alison B. Duxbury. Copyright 2004 by McGraw-Hill.*

northern seas. As so often happens, this union evolved through trade. By the 1100s Italian vessels regularly appeared in ports of Muslim Spain. The Genoese increased their presence and expanded into Atlantic shipping lanes when the rulers of the Kingdom of Castile conquered these ports in the 13th century. Sailing through the Strait of Gibraltar, Genoese merchants established a presence in Flanders and the English Isles. Italian traders traveling in galleys took luxury items (silks, metalwork, fruits, and spices) to the northern seas and traded them for wool, cloth, and tin. The Venetians closely followed the Genoese into the Atlantic Ocean, with Castilians and Portuguese following a few decades later. In the northern seas, the Mediterranean sailors encountered the Hanseatic League, a powerful trade confederacy comprising more than 200 towns, including the famed Lübeck, Danzig, and Riga that had thrived initially on the Baltic Sea's herring trade.

The rough northern seas of the Atlantic provided a stimulus for seaworthy vessels. Toward the end of the Middle Ages, Hanseatic traders had replaced the longboats of the Norsemen with the cog, a wide, spacious type of transport ship that used a steering oar as rudder. The northern cog proved to be an inspiration for Mediterranean traders, whose carracks were equally sturdy but employed different construction methods. The product of the interchange of northern and Mediterranean maritime ideas was the caravel, which adopted novel construction. Shipbuilders opted to construct the ship's frame first, allowing for thicker planking than the carrack. Similarly, the caravel could carry triangular or lateen sails, the latter an adoption from the Indian Ocean. In addition to the lateen sail, the Indian Ocean contributed tools such as the astrolabe, to determine a ship's latitude, and the Chinese magnetic compass. Thus the technology that made transatlantic voyages possible drew upon navigational innovations from across the Eurasian world.

European motives for expansion are frequently described as wealth, conversion of heathen peoples, and individual and national fame (better known as gold, God, and glory). The lust for gold, partially prompted by an expanding European economy, was what first lured Mediterranean peoples to West African shores. The wealth of the Kingdom of Mali, for instance, was legendary. The Catalan atlas of 1375 (see chapter 1) depicts King Mansa Musa wearing a golden crown and holding a softball-sized gold nugget in his hand. Generous with his gold on his pilgrimage to Mecca, this king single-handedly depressed the price of this precious metal for several decades. Moreover, the regions below the Sahara desert promised an ample supply of slaves for the Mediterranean.

Westward expansion into the Atlantic Ocean was much more haphazard than expansion into the northern seas. A perennial problem was the return voyage against unfavorable currents and winds. The charting of the Azores, the Canaries, and the island of Madeira became crucial in this matter. Genoese mariners were the first to venture into these regions. Cautiously looking out for favorable winds and currents, they reached the Canary Islands, inhabited by the Guanches, in the early 1300s. Mediterranean mariners had apparently reached the islands before, but sustained contact failed to materialize for the same reasons that would frustrate the Genoese: the return voyage. Adverse currents and winds made the Canaries a difficult point to reach. When the plague ravaged the Italian peninsula by the 1350s, the Genoese put an end to active exploration. But other European maritime powers did not forget about them, and the islands played a crucial role in Castilian and Portuguese expansion into the eastern Atlantic Ocean. The Portuguese, for instance, would reach the Azores in the 1420s and quickly realize the importance of these islands. Located on the same latitude as Lisbon, though at a considerable distance from either North Africa or the Iberian Peninsula, these islands assured anyone who reached them of favorable westerly winds that would carry them quickly and safely to familiar shores. The Portuguese labeled this the *volta do mar*, the return through the sea. The Genoese continued their involvement in these endeavors, not only providing important financial resources for the Portuguese crown, but also introducing sugar cane from the eastern shores of the Mediterranean; it became a lucrative crop on the strategic island of Madeira.

Portuguese exploration is often associated with the name of Dom Henrique, better known in the English language as Prince Henry the Navigator, who was the third son of King João of Portugal. This term is ill-chosen at best and did not appear in writing until several centuries following his passing. Indeed, during his lifetime Henrique did no more than two short water crossings, and none of these fell outside the sheltered waters of the Mediterranean. His title hails more from his chroniclers' extolling than from any actual nautical accomplishments. Henrique was above all a practical man who, after realizing his dim chances of attaining the Portuguese crown, developed a keen interest in commercial success. Economic opportunities, rather than a complex vision of a Portuguese empire, governed his decision making. Within these parameters, however, he did encourage the colonization of the Azores and the island of Madeira to boost the sugar industry developing in these islands. Furthermore, Genoese agents sailing in his name went up the

Gambia and Senegal rivers to make contact with the Mali Empire. It also was under his tutelage that mariners finally rounded the dreaded Cape Bojador and proceeded to the African West Coast. In short, Dom Henrique's commercial vision led to further expansion. After Henrique's death in 1460, the Portuguese continued to expand along the coast of Africa, establishing a number of prominent fortifications. The Portuguese quickly learned that along the rugged African coast, diseases and well-armed opponents prevented easy conquests. Accommodation rather than confrontation thus determined the protocol of Henrique's descendants. Several commercial treaties with West African societies followed initial exploration, most of them styled after the Genoese example in the Mediterranean. Portuguese merchants and agents established themselves in strategic African port cities, frequently intermarrying with the indigenous population. Developing fluencies in local languages, they soon became important middlemen in the nascent Portuguese-African trade.

Historians frequently ponder the question of why Castile and Portugal led the expansive Atlantic venture, and not France and Genoa. France, for instance, had a larger population than Portugal and Spain combined, and her coastal areas gave access to the Atlantic as well as the Mediterranean. Supply lines played an important decision in this case, as France's distance to the Canaries and the Bulge of Africa was further than the Iberian Peninsula's. Genoa, on the other hand, greatly influenced the nascent economies of Castile and Portugal, but her merchants and bankers preferred to create financial rather than political empires. This was the case, for instance, in Seville. When Castilian monarchs took this strategic city from Muslim rule in 1248, they invited Genoese merchants and bankers to anchor its economic role in the emerging Mediterranean Atlantic. The Genoese represented a powerful trade diaspora in this city as they became instrumental in Castilian westward expansion. Excluded by treaty (Alcobaça 1479) from the gold-yielding coasts of West Africa, Castilian monarchs scrambled for alternatives. With the backing of Italian bankers, a new Spanish monarchy (emerging out of the union of the kingdoms of Castile and Aragon) was able to dislodge the last Muslim stronghold, located in Granada, in 1492. The same year the Spanish monarchs decided to sponsor a Genoese sailor by the name of Christopher Columbus to take three caravels across the Atlantic.

The story of Columbus's encounter with the New World is well known. His readings of important travel accounts (chiefly those by Marco

Polo, see chapter 1) led him to believe that some islands off the coast of Asia were only 2,080 miles from the Canaries, when in reality they were closer to 12,000 miles away. Columbus built upon the expertise of Mediterranean sailors who had discovered easterly winds off the coast of Madeira that propelled him to the Americas. He made landfall on an island of the Bahamas chain, which he named San Salvador. His voyage became a fateful one, and historians have bequeathed his name to the biological and cultural exchanges following 1492.

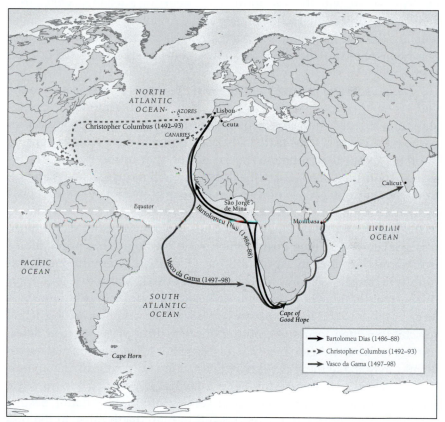

FIGURE 2-2   PORTUGUESE AND SPANISH EXPANSIONS INTO THE ATLANTIC OCEAN

Source: Used with permission from Traditions and Encounters (2nd ed.), by Jerry H. Bentley and Herbert F. Ziegler. Copyright 2002 by McGraw-Hill.

COLUMBIAN EXCHANGES

DISEASES

The opening of the Atlantic world involved important interchanges between Africa, the Americas, and Europe. While Eurasia and Africa had been in contact for a millennium, the Americas were always a world apart. Extensive trade networks linked the peoples of the Americas, as did such large-scale empires as the Aztecs and Incas. Yet contact with other continents was limited. Two exceptions are confirmed Viking settlements on the American Atlantic coast and assumed Polynesian arrival on the Pacific side (see chapter 3). Important as these contacts may have been, they hardly compare with the transformations occurring after 1492, which triggered a new unit of interaction known as the Atlantic world. The spread of animals, diseases, peoples, and plants, as well as ideas and wealth, from one hemisphere to the other is known collectively as the Columbian Exchange.

The most tragic of these transfers was the export of diseases from the Old World (Europe and Africa) to the New World (Americas). Understanding disease transfers requires insights into the operation of pathogens. There is some truth to the assertion that certain environments are more lethal than others. While it is true that in the tropics, for instance, continued exposure to the direct sun will induce sickness and ultimately death, the types of diseases that such environments harbor is even more important. Even in similar environments, the degree and type of diseases may differ as they can change quickly in response to immunities developed by their hosts' community. The degree of a population's isolation determines the specialization of its disease environment. Immunity is mostly acquired rather than inherited. Many diseases occur during childhood, which determines the adult population's immunity. A large number of childhood diseases, smallpox for instance, are less lethal for children than for adults. But inheritance does play a part in determining immunity. Again childhood is important. The genetic makeup of a child may make the difference between life and death during an outbreak. Similarly, those children with a favorable genetic code may live long enough to pass it on to the next generation. In the Atlantic Basin a relative degree of isolation would result in high death rates. In the pre-Columbian Atlantic, one can isolate roughly three distinct disease environments. Asia, North Africa, and Europe stood in contact with each other for the better part of a millennium. European populations had developed immunities to the most common Eurasian diseases. Sub-Saharan

Africa, a second disease environment, had the whole gamut of temperate diseases, but added to that a whole array of tropical diseases—yellow fever, sleeping sickness, and the more lethal *falciparum* variety of malaria, to mention but a few. The third disease environment could be found in the Americas, where the populations had little exposure to or immunity from diseases emerging from both Eurasia and tropical Africa. The effect of these interchanges was felt quickly in some of the islands that became launching pads for future exploration. While the Azores, Madeira, and the Cape Verde Islands were not populated, the Canaries supported an estimated population of 80,000 to 100,000 in the year 1400. This population, called Guanches, was probably related to nomadic populations in North Africa, but had lost its ties to these mainland societies centuries ago. Though they were organized in only small kingdoms and fought with rudimentary weapons, the Guanches put up a fierce fight against the arriving southern Europeans. Their worst enemy, however, was introduced diseases, and they unwittingly became the biological test case for the Americas. The last campaign against an already weakened Guanche population occurred in 1496, with the effect of almost complete extinction.

When Columbus's ships reached the Bahamas in October of 1492, they reached a world that was as rich and varied as Eurasia. Isolated from Africa and Eurasia for many thousand years, the peoples of the Americas had developed over 2000 languages and had adapted to virtually all environments. The Americans had domesticated a series of animals and plants. The food crops they developed were equal if not superior to those from Eurasia. In terms of animals, however, North and South America were comparatively lacking. While barkless dogs became important hunting companions, and llamas and alpacas served as beasts of burden in the Andes, the absence of a greater variety of domesticated animals triggered a smaller disease pool. Scientists argue that mammal disease agents are frequently zoonotic, meaning they can be transmissible between humans and animals. In Eurasia, an existing larger pool of domesticated animals allowed for a greater rate of interspecies infections. In the Americas such diseases occurred less frequently. This is not to say that the Americas were a disease-free environment; rather, a number of skin and even respiratory diseases afflicted Native American peoples. Yet nothing prepared them for the arrival of European diseases following Columbus's wake.

Much has been written about the mortality rate in the Americas, and the debates are still raging. In the absence of complete pre-Columbian censuses, most historians operate with informed guesses to arrive at the contact population estimates. Conservative investigators estimate the Americas' population at 20 to 25 million. Recent suggestions, however, propose in excess of 100 million. Whatever the size of this population, the impact of infectious diseases was devastating. The hardest hit were the populations inhabiting the tropical lowlands of the Americas. Native Americans in these regions had to contend with European diseases such as smallpox and measles, as well as respiratory infections such as pneumonia and whooping cough. Adding to this were diseases from the tropical regions of the Old World, including malaria as well as dengue and yellow fever. The result was that the indigenous Arawaks and Caribs of the Caribbean islands perished within a century of Columbus's arrival. Similar mortality rates occurred along the tropical coastal areas of South America. The lone exception to this were the Maya people of the Yucatan peninsula, whose mortality rates were lower, possibly due to the absence of the anopholes mosquito carrier of the malaria pathogen. Similarly, the populations of the cooler highlands of South America experienced lower mortality rates since they experienced devastating pathogens only from Europe, not the imported tropical diseases from Africa. A few estimates illustrate the difference between highland and lowland mortality. The pathogens had a dramatic effect in Mexico, where an estimated population of 11 million at contact in 1519 fell to one million by about 1600—a decline of over 90 percent. In the highlands of Spanish Peru, the numbers were significant (about 50–60 percent decline), but less radical than in the tropical regions.

On the African continent, things were different. The kingdoms of West Africa had been exposed to Eurasian diseases through trans-Saharan trade routes. So, when the Portuguese arrived along the coast of Africa, the diseases they brought were far less lethal. Also, the tropical diseases of sub-Saharan Africa did not fare well in the milder climates of the Mediterranean Sea. So while the Mediterranean Atlantic provided the Saharan Atlantic with its pathogens, the reverse did not occur. Consequently, European populations were spared the more lethal varieties of malaria as well as the devastating effects of dengue and yellow fever. However, Europeans reaching tropical Africa suffered mortality rates similar to those of the New World. The alarming death rates partially prevented large-scale European settlements in Africa. Where diseases became an unintended but effective weapon of conquest in the Americas, they became an element in the defense of sub-Saharan Africa from European incursions.

POWER

The transatlantic spread of disease greatly assisted the conquest and imposition of Spanish and, as far as Brazil is concerned, Portuguese power over the Americas. The first Spanish presence emerged in the Caribbean, where authorities established small colonies on Santo Domingo, Cuba, and Jamaica. By 1520, however, the incentive of rich mineral deposits proved too much to resist. A military class, generally known as *conquistadores* (or conquerors) set out to establish their fame and Spanish rule on the mainlands of the Americas. While gold was an important motivating factor, religion became a means of justification for conquest. The result was the *requerimiento*, a ritual through which Spanish soldiers read out their rendition of Christianity to a bewildered crowd of Native Americans. When the Amerindians refused the offered baptism, the Spanish assumed that they had the legal right to subjugate the indigenous population. This process became even more pronounced when Martin Luther's Reformation of the Church spread through the northern lands of Europe.

Using Christianity as a legal foundation for conquest, the Spaniards toppled two important empires: the Aztecs and the Incas. Much has been made of the technological advantage of gunpowder and steel as well as the presence of horses unfamiliar to the Amerindians. While these items may have provided an advantage in the initial contact phases, it is doubtful whether they proved to be decisive in the conquest itself. The rapid Spanish success was probably the result of a combination of factors that included exploitation of divisions within the Amerindian population, hostage taking, technology, and the devastating effects of pathogens. By the second half of the 1500s, the Spaniards were in control of vast tracts of land located mostly in Central and South America.

Within the overthrown empires, the Spaniards sought to exploit existing hierarchies of power. The conquerors married into deposed royal families to gain legitimacy and received *encomiendas*, which were royal grants not in land but in people, required to work for their Spanish overlords. In the name of the absent Spanish royalty, the soldiers controlled communities of Native Americans, collecting tribute and theoretically providing Christian instruction. This position and the attendant privileges were usually abused.

Three factors provoked more direct royal involvement: the discovery of silver mines in Mexico and Peru, frequent missionary complaints of *encomendero* abuse, and the crown's desire to prevent the formation of a nobility in the Americas. The most important silver mine of Potosí (Bolivia) opened in 1544; two generations later, the surrounding city had 200,000 inhabitants, which made it larger than London or Paris. The Spanish crown faced growing expenditures as it was campaigning in Europe and the Mediterranean Sea against opponents including Ottoman Turks, Protestant reformers, and other royal regimes (especially France). The result was a rising demand for silver satisfied by the silver mines of the New World. Silver also established a vital link across the Pacific Ocean, where Spanish galleons met Chinese junks in the port of Manila (see chapter 3).

Religion had legitimized the conquest of the Americas, but it soon became an instrument through which to strip local *encomenderos* of their power. Spanish missionaries, faithful to their decision to gain converts among the Amerindians, deemed them *gente de razon* (people with reasoning capacities). Amerindians found their protector in a Dominican friar by the name of Bartolomé de Las Casas, who exposed the *encomenderos'* systematic abuse of power. Las Casas's writings became an integral component of a European defamatory campaign against the Spanish administration of the Americas. By 1550s, he won a major philosophical debate against an opponent who argued that Amerindians were less than humans. Less convinced by Las Casas's argument than by the need to control the flow of bullion, the Spanish crown actively intervened in the Americas and established a regime that was to last for over 200 years. The flow of centralized power across the Atlantic, however, would ultimately provide an incentive for rebellion.

ANIMALS AND PLANTS

In addition to diseases and power, animals too had an important impact on the New World. Abundant food supply and the relative absence of predators allowed Old World migrants from the animal world to multiply. Stowaways on European ships, such as the ever present rats, became a nuisance soon enough in environments where they quickly proceeded to outcompete indigenous varieties. European rats became a pest not just for a declining Amerindian population, but also for the growing European population in the New World. With ever increasing appetites, rats targeted not only introduced European grains but also native plants, contributing to or exacerbating existing food shortages.

Intentionally introduced animal species could be equally detrimental. Pigs and cattle became preferred animals in the New World. Europeans appreciated the hog for its omnivorous and self-replicating capabilities. Crew members left pigs on small islands of the Caribbean for a future supply of meat. Left to their own devices, pigs devastated both indigenous and introduced flora. Cattle were equally detrimental to the environment. Europeans desired cows for their ability to convert food unfit for human consumption, such as grass and leaves, into milk and meat. The other advantage of cattle over pigs was their adaptability to even arid environments. On the detrimental side, cattle contributed to the deforestation and ultimate erosion of land in the New World. As such, they contributed to the spread of Eurasian weeds unintentionally introduced alongside grains.

The introduction of the horse was the most beneficial for the indigenous peoples of the Americas. The story is well known, but worth repeating. Extinct in the Americas for almost 10,000 years, the horse was reintroduced in the New World by arriving Spaniards. Feral horses became a pest on the east coast of North America, but indigenous peoples spread them, via raids or trading, across the Great Plains of North America, where they transformed Native American societies. Between the early 1600s and the late 1700s, the introduction and domestication of horses by Native Americans became commonplace and frequently pre-dated European arrival. The Navajo and Zuni tribes, for instance, probably had horses by 1600; 100 years later, the frontier had reached the Shoshone in Idaho.

While Europeans provided many animals to the New World, the Americas became a prime supplier of plants rather than animals. Turkeys crossed the Atlantic from the Americas to the Old World, but had a lesser impact than American plants, including maize and the potato. Europeans were slow in accepting the advantage of the new crops. Originally cultivated by Mesoamericans, Europeans often rejected maize for its odd shape and peculiar taste. Five decades after Columbus's first trip, however, maize gained popularity for its ability to grow on relatively resource-poor soil with minimal precipitation. Similarly, corn could be stored for several years, and its byproducts, including leaves, were used for animal fodder. When the Spanish Inquisition pushed "infidels" out of Spain, fleeing Muslims introduced maize among their host societies in North Africa and the Middle East. The potato, on the other hand, was a relative latecomer to the Old World. It was not until the fall of the Inca Empire following the 1540s that potatoes found their way across the Atlantic. Mediterranean climates did not provide similar growing environments, delaying the potato's triumph by several decades. Once the potato was introduced to northern European climate zones, its cultivators soon realized the potential of this tuber. High-yielding crops, requiring less than one-third of the acreage required for grain production, and underground protection from frost and fungus secured the potato a prominent place in European diets.

On the surface, it is certain that New World crops had an important impact on the "old" regions of Africa, Asia, and Europe. Maize and potatoes greatly contributed to population growth in these regions through their high-yielding output. On the other hand, there may have been some negative social connotations as well. The low acreage requirements of these plants allowed the establishment of smaller plots, hence cementing class distinctions between rich landowners and poor farmers and retarding social upheavals and land distribution—most prominently in Ireland. Likewise, the reliance on such high-yielding crops encouraged monoculture, or the reliance on a single crop, and led to dietary-related illnesses and famines. Ireland serves as a well-established example. The introduction of the potato was instrumental in doubling the population; Ireland's population in 1750 was barely 3 million, but by 1841 it had reached the critical number of 8 million. The same year, an American parasite affecting potatoes in the New World was introduced into the Old World, with dire consequences. Although potato crops were failing throughout Europe, the results were nowhere more severe than in Ireland, where the reliance on potatoes was most pronounced. Over the next decade, roughly one million people died as a consequence of the famine. Millions more chose to emigrate, some to England, others across the Atlantic, figuring thus as an important part of the Irish diaspora. The Irish case, much like Eurasian diseases affecting Native American populations ealier, well illustrates how these biological interchanges connected the Old and the New World in unintended yet tragic ways.

One plant involved in the Columbian Exchanges changed Atlantic Ocean economics forever: sugarcane. First introduced to the Mediterranean from Asia via the Crusades, sugar cane quickly gained in popularity and became a major crop on the Mediterranean islands. With the Iberian expansion, cane was brought to Madeira, and by 1493, the Americas. The Spaniards' attempts to sustain sugarcane in the Caribbean floundered partially due to a labor shortage resulting from pandemics and the intense focus on mineral extraction from Mexico and Peru. The Portuguese, on the other hand, utilized their Brazilian territories, devoid of minerals, for sugar plantations so heavily that by the 1570s sugar surpassed exotic woods as a major export item. Native Americans first met the labor-intensive requirements of cane cultivation, but the Portuguese soon supplanted them with African slaves when the Native Americans' numbers declined. Not only did the Portuguese have unrestricted access to the West African coast, but the voyages from Angola to Brazil, via the Atlantic seascapes, took less than half the time than from Africa to the Caribbean.

AFRICAN MIGRATIONS TO THE AMERICAS

Sugar cane fueled a developing plantation industry that in turn caused one of the largest migrations in human history: the African slave trade. While Europeans also migrated to the New World, their numbers stayed well below that of the Africans until the 1840s. It was from that date to the outbreak of the Great War in 1914 that Europeans replaced Africans as the largest human migration (see chapter 4). The origins of the transatlantic slave trade are connected to the unintentional decline in indigenous societies and the emergence of a labor-intensive plantation complex in the Americas. The resilience of African workers, the existence of slavery and slave markets in Africa, and the European presence along the African coast, likewise facilitated the Atlantic slave trade.

When the Portuguese returned their first cargo of African slaves in 1444 from northern Mauritania, their economic importance was secondary only to gold. The Portuguese were continuing a tradition: the import of slaves to the Mediterranean Sea. The trans-Saharan slave trade had established this pattern centuries ago, and the Portuguese were

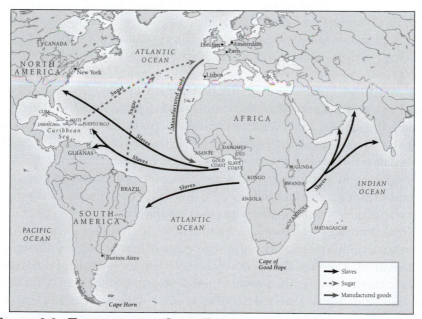

FIGURE 2-3   TRANSATLANTIC SLAVE TRADE
Source: Used with permission from Traditions and Encounters (2nd ed.), by Jerry H. Bentley and Herbert F. Ziegler. Copyright 2002 by McGraw-Hill.

helping themselves to one of the items traded along this route, cutting out the middlemen and increasing their profits. The Spanish and Portuguese had used slave labor before, in particular Africans, Guanches (from the Canary Islands), and Muslims. The combination, however, of an extreme labor-intensive industry in the Americas and a declining native population gave slavery a hitherto unknown dimension. Faced with declining numbers of indigenous peoples, the Spanish crown decided against a permanent enslavement of Native Americans. Nor could the relatively small population of Spain (roughly seven million by 1550) or Portugal (roughly one million during the same time period) alleviate the labor situation. Spain was able to draw on established corvee (nonpaid) labor patterns used by indigenous empires and societies (especially those of the Incas in the Andes mountains and the Aztecs in Mesoamerica). The Portuguese possessions on the other hand could not employ the more loosely organized Tupi-Guarani (an important Native American language family spoken in Brazil, Paraguay, and Uruguay) confederacies for the same purpose. Similarly, as the numbers of African slaves in the New World grew, Europeans realized that Africans had resistance to tropical diseases and Eurasian pathogens. Although exact numbers are unknown, it is estimated that European mortality in the Caribbean was four times higher than that of African slaves. Such resilience did not remain unnoticed and provided additional impetus for the trade.

The Portuguese had a theoretical advantage over the Spaniards in the slave trade. A papal bull in 1493, modified by a treaty (signed at Tordesillas) a year later, divided the Atlantic between the Spaniards and Portuguese along a north–south line running through the ocean roughly 370 leagues west of the Cape Verde Islands. This agreement is often seen as an important step toward establishing a viable law of the sea and of boundaries delineating global seascapes. In practice, however, the pope granted merely an agenda for the religious conversion of indigenous peoples, not a road map for imperial conquest of the ocean. The English, Dutch, and French frequently infringed this arbitrary boundary.

The Portuguese, however, were unable to impose their rule on African societies that could supply the needed manpower for emerging Brazilian plantations. So the Portuguese tried to rework the existing African slave trade in their favor. They soon realized, however, that accommodation rather than open conflict was a more appropriate means to acquire desired human cargos. The Portuguese consequently settled in uninhabited delta islands or coastal regions, where they established outposts and forts, often referred to as factories. Any conquest of African regions was immediately out of the question. High death rates from yellow fever and malaria prevented a high concentration of troops. Similarly, African warriors quickly adapted to European military technology and responded in kind. Any possible European advantage evaporated with the introduction of cavalry in African societies. Although willing to use force, the Europeans had only limited means to compel African states to increase the volume of slave trade. When the Kingdom of Benin, for instance, decided in 1516 to restrict the export of male slaves, Europeans could do little else but look for a new supplier. Any conquest of vast African territories had to wait until the second half of the 1800s, when the slave trade was largely over.

How is one to assess the impact of the transatlantic slave trade on the African continent? One way of doing so is to compare the African migration with that of Europeans. Given the involuntary nature of the African migration, it is easy to understand that return movement from the Americas back to Africa was virtually nonexistent. With Europeans, on the other hand, return migration accounted for an estimated 50 percent of all migrants. This meant that the 10 to 12 million individuals who left Africa on board the slave ships between 1500 and 1850, not to mention the many millions lost in capture or transit, were permanently lost to the continent. Furthermore, sex and age discrimination of the slaves favored young over old and men over women. This meant that Europeans extracted a large percentage of Africa's labor force. While generalizations are difficult, the impact of these demographics in limiting African population growth is beyond doubt. But the import of American plants to Africa had triggered a population increase similar to that experienced by Asia and Europe. The introduction of manioc, a tuberous edible root that is the source of tapioca, from Brazil to African rainforests revolutionized agriculture in the tropical regions. Similarly, agriculture in the African savannas gained immensely from the introduction of maize, although most historians now believe the impact to be uneven.

It is true that Africa became involved in an exchange system linking the continent with the Americas and Europe. Yet at the same time, the name given to this exchange system—triangular trade—refers more to an abstraction than to concrete reality. To graphically illustrate this exchange, historians superimpose a triangle upon the Atlantic Ocean. The first side of the triangle links Europe and Africa through the exchange of manufactured goods including cloth, guns, and liquor. These goods are then exchanged for slaves, whose trajectory through Atlantic seascapes to the Americas forms the second side of the triangle, known as the Middle

Passage. Upon their arrival in the Americas, the African slaves produce the raw materials (sugar, tobacco, cotton, etc.) that are then shipped to Europe in the last leg of the triangle.

Viewed from an African perspective, the situation is far more complex. It ignores, for instance, that slaves became a major commodity following the year 1600, replacing gold as a major African export item. It also ignores the Africans' ability to demand additional products from European arrivals and their successful resistance to the establishment of monopolies by European powers. The best example for this is the import of cowry shells to Africa. While this particular shell was known to African societies prior to the arrival of the Portuguese, it quickly became a major currency due to its durability. The Portuguese shipped most of these shells from the Maldive Islands, a set of coral atolls located in the Indian Ocean—linking two major oceans and suggesting additional "legs" to the exchange system. Demand for the shells quickly spread, and during the 1700s, it is estimated that British and Dutch mariners imported no less than 10 billion shells to the coast of West Africa. The arrival of such vast quantities of shells caused inflation among African societies, but also proved costly to the Europeans. In order to gain access to the desired goods, British and Dutch traders had to purchase the shells from Indian traders, who in turn had obtained them from inhabitants of the Maldives in exchange for rice and other foodstuffs not available in the atoll environments.

This is not to deny the disruptive implications of the slave trade. Warfare was indeed one of the main sources for slaves on the African continent. The presence of European slave traders facilitated armed conflict, and on occasion, provided the weapons involved. There are a number of well-documented cases in which slave trade provided incentives for state formation along the West Coast of Africa. Two of the best known are the Asante and the Kingdom of Dahomey.

The so-called Gold Coast along Africa's Gulf of Guinea hosted a comparatively large number of European settlements and forts. These had emerged as a consequence less of the trade in human beings than of the trade in gold. The pull of gold fields located in the interior stimulated state formations, and this region was also one of the first to adopt American crops (maize and manioc), which in turn allowed for a denser population concentration. This was the initial context for the Asante state, whose origins date to about 1680, when Osei Tutu pulled together a number of rival clans. By the 1700s, the Asante began conquering surrounding peoples, who were incorporated into this emerging kingdom. Their conquests also coincided with a shift in maritime trade. By the 1660s, the export of African slaves had risen in importance, and over the next two decades comprised 75 percent of all exports from this region. The Asante used the demand for gold and slaves to further their kingdom, which by 1820 spread over 250,000 square miles. The outer ring of their domain was composed of slave-providing tributary regions. The wealth generated from the slave trade supported the Asante state until the British conquest in the late 1800s.

While European demand for slaves provided an incentive for the growth of the Kingdom of Dahomey, the initial situation on the so-called Slave Coast (located on the Bight of Benin) was different from the Asante. There was no gold in this region; consequently there was no significant European presence in the area until about 1600. In the early 1700s Dahomey was first mentioned as a state of lesser importance in the hinterland of the Slave Coast. This peripheral location, however, provided Dahomey access to inland populations and the opportunity to take control of the slave trade. In the 1720s, Dahomey had conquered the major seaports along the Bight of Benin, giving them access to British slave traders. Adopting novel military technology to expand their domain, Dahomenian rulers became renowned for their strict militaristic rule. Traditional javelins and swords were abandoned for European muskets, and African warfare entered a new phase. Their military units included not only men, but also women, often described as the fabled Amazons by European observers. The destructiveness of the Dahomenian forces, however, was offset by their attempt to create a centralized system of rule over an area that was formerly fragmented. Dahomenian expansion created a bureaucracy and greater efficiency, and some scholars argue that such centralization was a constructive response to the disruption of slave trading. Dahomey continued to be a strong state until defeated by French forces in the 1890s.

The opening of the Atlantic Ocean by European explorers had tremendous implications for the peoples of the African continent. However, the control over these seascapes was a different issue altogether. The Portuguese–Spanish attempt to divide the ocean into two spheres of influence was largely imaginary. The Spanish had opened the first route, connecting the Caribbean to Europe, and had declared a monopoly, which they found difficult to maintain. The Portuguese were instrumental in opening a second route, from West Africa to Brazil, that became the crucial trajectory of the Middle Passage. English and French mariners were responsible for opening a third route, from Europe to Newfoundland (similar to the Vikings), where they found rich fishing grounds. None of these routes proved exclusive. The Spanish soon found out that their vital bullion link between the

New and Old worlds, known as the *Carrera de Indias*, attracted attention. Galleons loaded with gold and silver made their way from the mainland to the port of Havana in Cuba, and then sailed north to capture the Gulf Stream until reaching favorable westerlies to the Azores, to end their voyage in Seville. Timing was essential; any delay could bring about the beginning of the hurricane season (late August to October) and destroy valuable vessels. More dangerous than storms, however, were Dutch, English, and French privateers, or pirates operating in the service of the state. They inflicted heavy casualties among Spanish galleons and forced them to band together while traveling. Continuous conflict in the Atlantic and ongoing European wars forced the Spanish to sign treaties, which allowed England and France to establish colonies in areas not occupied by the Spanish. They were quickly joined by the Dutch, who asserted their independence from Habsburg Spain by intervening in the Atlantic trade. From their Caribbean bases, the Dutch not only drove the Portuguese out of the slave trade, but threatened to expel them from their Brazilian domains. Between 1630 and 1654, the Dutch controlled Brazil until Portuguese settlers regained control.

TRANSATLANTIC REVOLUTIONS

NORTH AMERICA

In the late 1700s, important revolutions erupted throughout the Atlantic realm. The American Revolution began in 1776 and ended in 1783; the French Revolution started in 1789 and did not come to a conclusion until the fall of Napoleon in 1815. The revolution in Saint Domingue began in 1791 and created a new nation, Haiti, in 1804. The Spanish dependencies in the New World were rocked with violence between the years 1809 and 1825, creating a number of new nations and leaving the Spanish government with only a smattering of colonies in the Caribbean. All of these revolutions influenced each other across the Atlantic Ocean.

The plantation economy of the New World had reached its height in the 1770s, owing to dramatic decreases in shipping costs and improvements in technology. In return, these connections stimulated and increased trade relations between Africa, Europe, and the New World. Overseas colonies absorbed a surplus European population, who were fed and strengthened by New World crops. With people came ideas, and none were more powerful than those of the Enlightenment. This movement, which owes much to the Pacific exchanges explored in the next chapter, sought the application of reason for the improvement of human society. The main proponents sought to increase equality, even if only among men, and advocated the safeguarding of certain inalienable rights. Some even had revolutionary ideas about slavery, and they were consequently ignored in the New World. Economic ideas also were key in the development of the Atlantic. In 1776, the same year as the American Revolution, Adam Smith published his famous work, *Wealth of Nations*. This had several implications for the Atlantic Ocean. Besides advocating limited government deregulation within international trade, Smith also deemed slavery as irrational and uneconomical. Free labor, he argued, was cheaper and more efficient than that supplied by slaves from Africa. The ripples of such ideas soon created wider circles of influence in the Atlantic world.

Enlightened ideas received further attention when metropolitan states involved themselves actively in their overseas colonies. By the eighteenth century, increase in military technology and administration had increased the cost of warfare. The availability of colonies also meant that European conflicts were exported overseas. Such was the case of the Seven Years War (1756–63). The war officially started when Prussian monarch Frederick II, a close ally of Great Britain, invaded neighboring Saxony in a preemptive strike. The conflict soon escalated when France and Austria signed an alliance in 1757 to defeat Prussia. When Great Britain rushed in to support its Prussian ally, the war ceased to be a mere European conflict. Along the colonial frontier in North America, French and British settlers had frequent skirmishes that dated back to unsettled differences following King George's War (1744–48). There were well over one million British settlers living along the east coast of North America, outnumbering their French counterparts by nearly 10 to 1. The British settlers experienced a degree of self-empowerment literally unmatched by all but a few individuals in the Old World. Land for tobacco, indigo, and rice cultivation provided Europeans with incentives that were lacking in the more severe climates of the French northern territories. British and French conflicts only increased after war broke out in Europe. Both the French and the British authorities enlisted their colonial settlers and Native Americans in the conflict. After initial French success, British troops moved on French Canada, defeating and occupying a number of prominent forts. The Treaty of Paris, signed in 1756, officially ended the war and left Great Britain with most of the French territories in North America. This victory proved costly, however, and the British monarch sought to raise taxes on the thirteen British colonies on the shores of the Atlantic Ocean.

The British attempt to cash in on the lucrative Atlantic colonies soon drew resentment. The American settlers expected little more than protection from the British crown. That wish would quickly change when more structured colonial administration grew following the Seven Years War. Imposed limitations on trade with French and Spanish colonies cut into profit margins, and new taxes imposed to shoulder the British Empire's cost only aggravated the situation. When the settlers chose armed confrontation and declared themselves independent in 1776, they adopted a self-conscious mix of Enlightenment ideas coming across the Atlantic Ocean. Humiliated by the peace treaty following the Seven Years War, French monarch Louis XVI sided with the Anglo-American revolutionaries. Spain and the Netherlands provided further support to the settlers, who, after initial setbacks, were able to score significant victories. Fearing greater loss to their colonial empire, British authorities sued for peace. In 1783, Great Britain granted independence to the original thirteen colonies. The revolution was successful in a political sense, but brought only limited change in society. The issue of slavery, for instance, was not solved, and the institution remained a thorn in the heart of the new country until 1865. Great Britain, on the other hand, recognized a need for change in North America and institutionalized more flexible and decentralized policies in Canada.

FRANCE AND HAITI

France also felt the impact of the American Revolution. Although the country emerged victorious through its alliance with the revolutionary settlers, the war also represented a further financial drain for the already overstretched resources of the French crown. King Louis XV (r. 1715–74) had already levied taxes following the disastrous Seven Years War. In his efforts, he did not exempt the French nobility, and the individuals composing this class now demanded a say in government. The French alliance with the American colonists proved equally costly, and the government of Louis XVI, who succeeded Louis XV, was facing bankruptcy. Under pressure from increasingly disgruntled nobility, Louis XVI decided to revive the Estates General, a political organization that had not met since 1614, when increasingly powerful French monarchs decided to rule without interference of others. This organization represented the French populace unevenly, as most French subjects (excluding nobility and clergy) were lumped into an undifferentiated third estate. The members of this estate quickly realized that Louis XVI was attempting to disenfranchise them by forming an alliance with the first (clergy) and the second (nobility) estates. They consequently walked out of the Estates General and formed their own political organization, the National Assembly, and asked the other estates to join them. Sensing mounting unrest, best expressed by the storming of an infamous political prison, known as the Bastille, on July 14, 1789, Louis XVI agreed to the demands of the National Assembly. France was on its way to becoming a constitutional monarchy, but events soon escalated. In comparison with the thirteen original colonies of America, the French Revolution was more radical in its intent and unleashed a flood of enlightened practices. Attempts at political manipulation failed, and King Louis XVI soon lost support, his country, and ultimately his head. While the political excesses of the French Revolution were soon contained, they translated into a protracted military campaign guided by Napoleon Bonaparte.

Across the Atlantic, the French Revolution had tremendous effects on the French colony of Saint Domingue. The island's fertile land produced two-fifths of the world's sugar and an overwhelming 40 percent of France's overseas trade. The colony's population was quite different, though, from that of the emerging United States of America. Almost 90 percent of its population were African slaves (close to 500,000) with the rest dividing themselves between Europeans (mostly French) and free Africans, many of them of mixed French and African ancestry, so-called mulattos. Mulattos and French settlers became increasingly disenchanted with French control over the colonial economy that dictated almost exclusive trade with France. The French settlers embraced the news of the revolution in their country in 1789, expecting this event to provide them with greater autonomy. Mulattos and freed African slaves, on the other hand, were bitterly disappointed when they found their access to the French National Assembly blocked by French settlers. Angered by this state of affairs, Mulattos joined by many African slaves, fought a protracted guerilla campaign. Their self-appointed leader was Toussaint-Louverture (ca. 1744–1803), who successfully resisted French settlers, British troops, and an invading force of French soldiers sent by Napoleon. To add insult to injury, in 1803, Napoleon also reversed the National Assembly's decree to abolish slavery in the French colonies. French troops cut down by yellow fever and African rebels conceded defeat in 1802, but tricked Toussaint Louverture into following them to France for negotiations. Captured and delivered to Napoleon, Toussaint died in prison a year later. One of his deputies, Jean-Jacques Dessalines, continued the struggle and proclaimed an independent Haiti, a name adopted from the decimated indigenous Arawak, meaning "mountainous land," in 1804. Haiti became, after the United States, the second independent republic in the Americas. The revolution casted long shadows. Fear of the implications of an African-led Haitian revolution induced other governments to place restrictive edicts in the Caribbean isles to keep slaves in check. Unlike the United States, Haitian leaders initially were unable to gain diplomatic recognition from prominent nations. France, for instance, did not officially recognize the country until three decades following the revolution, and only in exchange for 150 million francs in indemnities for the property lost to the French settlers. This sum of money put further restrictions on a country that was struggling to find its financial footing following a devastating campaign that had left at least 150,000 people dead. The main positive outcome was that the Haitian revolution accelerated already existing forces that would end the slave trade: the British abolished it in 1808 and the French in 1818.

SOUTH AMERICA

Napoleon's European campaigns also signaled the death knell for Spain's empire in the Americas. Tensions already existed in the empire before Napoleon's rise. A rigid *sociedad de castas*—caste society—placed severe constraints on social mobility, assigning each group (Africans, Mestizos, Native Americans, and Spaniards) a fixed position in the empire. Even among Spaniards there were distinctions. Fearful of losing control over Spanish possessions in the New World, the Spanish crown had entrusted most of the important political posts to European-born Spaniards (called *Peninsulares*). Spaniards born in the New World (called *Creoles*) staffed the growing bureaucracy, but were carefully excluded from politically influential offices. *Creoles*, however, were avid readers of Enlightenment ideas and closely followed the developments of the American War of Independence. Adding to this state of affairs was the careful monopoly over trade. The supply of hides, coffee, and tobacco from the American colonies greatly outstripped the meager Spanish market, and though industrializing Britain as well as the United States of America could have easily absorbed the surpluses, the Spanish crown kept a tight watch over such transactions. On the losing end of the Seven Years War, Spanish monarch Charles III (r. 1759–88) lifted trading restrictions somewhat by providing access to more Spanish ports besides Cadiz and Seville. On the whole, however, he remained suspicious of Creole ambition, opting instead to keep political power in the hand of trusted and loyal *Peninsulares*.

Events spun out of control when Napoleon invaded the Iberian Peninsula following 1807 and placed his brother on the throne of both Portugal and Spain. The Portuguese royal family narrowly escaped to Brazil, moving the capital of the Portuguese empire there. João IV (r. 1816–26) returned to assume the Portuguese crown following French occupation. His son Pedro soon declared Brazil independent from Portugal in 1822. Developments in Spanish-speaking parts of Latin America took a different turn. In the wake of Napoleon's occupation, Spanish royal power vanished altogether. This disorder led to disturbances in the Spanish colonies and the call for greater autonomy. Spanish officials, still suffering French occupation, in haste drew up a constitution in 1812 that, among other things, sought to address impending uprisings in the colonial territories of the Americas. It called for the abolition of the *sociedad de castas* and forced labor and provided for universal franchise for all men—however, excluding Africans. When the returning Spanish monarchy sought to eliminate this constitution, conflict spread. Two *Creoles*, José de San Martín (1778–1850) and Simón Bolívar (1783–1830), set out to fight Spanish loyalists in South America. The loyalists held out until the 1820s, but ultimately Spanish rule was effectively eliminated from the mainland of the Americas, thus completing 50 years of Atlantic revolutions.

CONCLUSION

Far from being an exclusively European artifact, the Atlantic involved the actions of a great many peoples on both sides of the Atlantic. Europeans instigated the flow of animals, diseases, ideas, and plants in the Atlantic Ocean between 1500 and 1800, but they could hardly predict the outcome. Exchanges in disease produced demographic shifts that reduced the indigenous populations of the Americas. Africans, and later Europeans, arrived in great numbers—the former as slaves, the latter mostly as free individuals. A deeply connected Atlantic world emerged, resulting in the development of strong states on both sides of the ocean. Individuals residing in the Americas imported the ideas of prominent Enlightenment philosophers that soon would give rise to revolutions throughout the Atlantic world. These revolutions, coupled with the tremendous migration of peoples from Africa and Europe, shaped the modern world and the consciousness of the people residing on both sides of the Atlantic Ocean. Atlantic experiences were crucial in the formation of new identities that could result in national expressions (as in the case of the United States) or a decisively transatlantic feeling (as developed among the descendants of African slaves). Following the 1800s, the Atlantic remained an important arena for the development of identities and novel technologies.

SUGGESTED READINGS

A good overview of a number of important articles on Atlantic history is Thomas Benjamin, Timothy Hall, and David Rutherford, eds., *The Atlantic World in the Age of Empire* (Boston: Houghton Mifflin, 2001). A recent rendition of Atlantic history, albeit from a decisively European angle, is Paul Butel's *The Atlantic* (New York: Routledge, 1999). For an alternative view of the Atlantic system, consult John Thornton, *Africa and the Africans in the Making of the Atlantic World*, 2nd ed. (New York: Cambridge University Press, 1998). The first chapter of this work, "The Birth of the Atlantic World," is a classic in terms of delineating the possibilities and constraints of the Atlantic Ocean and is balanced in considering all parties involved, including southern Europeans, West Africans, and the indigenous peoples of the Caribbean. Equally interesting is David Northrup's *The African Discovery of Europe, 1450–1850* (New York: Oxford University Press, 2002). Northrup skillfully reverses the perspective of European-African encounters to explore the African side of the equation. For an interesting European prelude to the Atlantic world, see Felipe Fernández-Armesto, *Before Columbus: Exploration and Colonization from the Mediterranean to the Atlantic, 1229–1492* (Philadelphia: University of Pennsylvania Press, 1987). Barry Cunliffe, *Facing the Ocean: The Atlantic and Its People 8000 BC–AD 1500* (New York: Oxford University Press, 2001), is an interesting and richly illustrated work on the early phase of Atlantic expansion from a Western perspective. David Kirby and Merja-Liisa Hinkkanen's work on *The Baltic and the North Sea* (New York: Routledge, 2000) has some interesting chapters on ship constructions in the northern seas of the Atlantic. For the intellectual challenge of "discovery" for the European mind, consult Anthony Grafton's *New World, Ancient Texts: The Power of Tradition and the Shock of Discovery* (Cambridge, MA: Belknap Press, 1992). On trade diasporas in Africa and elsewhere, consult Philip Curtin, *Cross-Cultural Trade in World History* (New York: Cambridge University Press, 1984). On biological exchanges, consult Alfred Crosby's *The Columbian Exchange: Biological and Cultural Consequences of 1492* (Westport, CT: Greenwood Press, 1972) and his *Ecological Imperialism: The Biological Expansion of Europe, 900–1200* (New York: Cambridge University Press, 1986). For the different disease environments, read Philip Curtin's classic article "Epidemiology and the Slave Trade," *Political Science Quarterly* 83 (1968): 190–216. For the spread of plantations through the Atlantic world, see Philip Curtin, *The Rise and Fall of the Plantation Complex: Essays in Atlantic History*, 2nd ed. (New York: Cambridge University Press, 1998). The impact of sugar on the

Atlantic Basin is best explored in Sydney Mintz, *Sweetness and Power* (New York: Penguin, 1986). An important compendium addressing many issues directly relevant to the Middle Passage is Herbert S. Klein's *The Atlantic Slave Trade* (New York: Cambridge University Press, 1999). Elizabeth Macke in her article "Early Modern Expansion and the Politicization of Oceanic Space," *Geographical Review* 89 (1999): 225–236, explores the implication of European exploration in the context of newfound liquid spaces. There is a literal explosion in the literature dealing with the African diaspora; a good starting point continues to be Joseph E. Harris, ed., *Global Dimensions of the African Diaspora*, 2nd ed. (Washington, DC: Howard University Press, 1993).

CHAPTER THREE TIMELINE

About 25,000 years ago	Settlement of Near Oceania
3000 BCE to 1000 CE	Settlement of Remote Oceania
1000–1500	Large-scale exchange networks in the Pacific Ocean
1519–21	Magellan's circumnavigation
1565	Andrés de Urdaneta finds a way to return from Asia to the Americas
1635	Japanese isolation policy
1768–80	James Cook's three voyages employ new ways of cartography
1787–1825	Height of the fur trade
1788	Convict settlement at Botany Bay (Sydney)
1815	Last Manila galleon voyage
1800–1865	Height of whaling industry

CHAPTER THREE

EXPLORING EXCHANGES IN THE PACIFIC OCEAN

GETTING STARTED ON CHAPTER THREE: How did Austronesian voyagers settle the islands of the Pacific Ocean? What prompted Spanish and Portuguese exploration of the Pacific? How did European exploration integrate the regions located along the Pacific Rim? How did geographical imaginations influence exploration? How did encounters between different cultures shape the Pacific world?

CHAPTER OUTLINE

INTRODUCTION

The Pacific Ocean is the largest body of water of this planet. Twice the size of the Atlantic, its history of exploration and integration is a curious one. Austronesian speakers braved the vast watery expanses separating the many islands of the Pacific at the same time they were expanding into the Indian Ocean during the first millennium before the birth of Christ. Yet unlike in the Indian Ocean, existing exchanges remained regional and did not span the whole Pacific Basin. European expansion following 1519 linked the Americas with Asia, yet did not fully integrate the Pacific until novel nautical instruments, such as the maritime chronometer, permitted such in the late 1700s. The cultural exchanges that followed in the wake of this integration changed both European and Pacific societies.

ORIGINAL SETTLEMENT OF THE PACIFIC ISLANDS

The settlement of the Pacific island world, also known as Oceania, has been controversial. First and foremost, scholars argue over the point of origin of the Pacific Islanders. Second, the same scholars have in the past questioned the navigational abilities of these people. Much of the controversy emerges from the sheer size of the Pacific Ocean and the distances separating the islands located in its basin. The Pacific is the world's largest and deepest ocean, spanning about one-third of the world's surface. Nearly twice the size of the Atlantic, its area of approximately 64,000,000 square miles (166,000,000 square kilometers) can easily accommodate all seven continents. As the name indicates, Oceania is by and large a waterlogged world; its roughly 10,000 islands range from New Guinea, earth's second-largest island, to the Republic of Kiribati (formerly the Gilbert Islands), with a land surface of a mere 275 square miles (or less than New York City). Perhaps the most astonishing fact about this watery world is that most of the islands surveyed by archaeologists show at least a trace of human habitation prior to 1500 CE.

The first clue to settlement derived from prevailing wind and ocean current directions. With the exception of the area around the large islands of Australia and New Zealand, wind patterns in the Pacific are fairly regular. Strong west-blowing winds are prevalent almost all year round north of about 25 degrees latitude and south of 27 degrees latitude. The eastern parts of the Pacific experience strong trade winds, which blow from a northeastern direction north of the equator and a southeastern direction south of the equator. In the island world of the Pacific, these trade winds are most prominent from May to September and serve to moderate the tropical climates with cooling breezes. In the western Pacific, monsoons occur due to the periodic heating and cooling of the Asian landmasses. While they are most prevalent in insular Southeast Asia (Indonesia and the Philippines, see chapter 1), they can be felt as far east as the Solomon Islands. In synchronicity, the ocean's currents mirror wind patterns. To the north of the equator currents flow clockwise, while to the south they flow counterclockwise, following the wind's northeastern and southeastern directions. Generally speaking, winds and currents generally blow and flow from the Americas to Asia, thus suggesting but not determining directions of settlement.

Despite prominent European eighteenth-century explorers attesting to the nautical ability of Pacific Islanders, many doubtful voices emerged in the second half of the 1900s. The assertion that Pacific Islanders simply drifted from the Americas into the area gained strength when the late adventurer Thor Heyerdahl traveled with a trusted crew from the coast of Peru to the Tuamotus in French Polynesia in 1947. Drifting from the Americas did not require extensive navigational knowledge, and some scholars leaped on the argument. There were those who argued that Polynesians even lacked the proper knowledge to navigate much beyond their home islands. While this may have been enough to settle islands in close proximity to their point of departure, critics asserted that the more distant settlements (such as Easter Island or the Hawaiian archipelago) came as a result of accident, not deliberation. By the 1960s the theory most widely accepted held that Polynesians had originated in the Americas and had drifted into the Pacific. A concerted effort by archaeologists and anthropologists, however, reversed this opinion over the next two decades. A combination of archaeological, ethnographic, linguistic, and experimental research subsequently and conclusively proved that the original Pacific Islanders not only possessed the skills and instruments to cross vast gaps of ocean, but also pointed at Asia rather than the Americas as the point of origin. Two crucial elements helped solve the puzzle. One was a particular decorated type of pottery called "Lapita," which, ranging from New Guinea to Samoa, became an archaeological footprint of the first Pacific migrants. Second, one of the last individuals trained in traditional navigation guided a double-hulled canoe from Hawai'i to Tahiti in 1976 without using any western technology. This 2,000-mile voyage was ample testimony of the first settlers' abilities.

The settlement of the Pacific occurred in two stages. Distinguishing between these two waves of settlers, archaeologists prefer to divide the

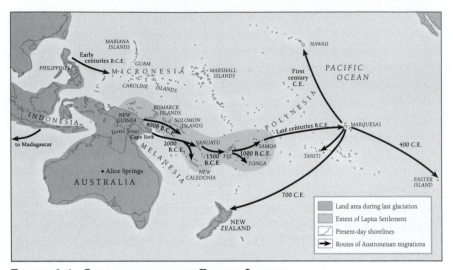

FIGURE 3-1   SETTLEMENT OF THE PACIFIC ISLANDS
Source: Used with permission from Traditions and Encounters (2nd ed.), by Jerry H. Bentley and Herbert F. Ziegler. Copyright 2002 by McGraw-Hill.

Pacific into a Near and a Remote Oceania. The first settlement occurred during the Pleistocene era. This era, which is better known as the Ice Age, lasted from two million to about 12,000 years ago. Widespread glaciation generally lowered sea levels and a landmass known as Sahul linked New Guinea with Australia. Relatively small water gaps of about 100 miles separated Sahul from Sunda (a landmass linking Southeast Asia). This prevented the earliest representatives of the human family, especially *Homo erectus*, from reaching Sahul. But by 50,000 to 40,000 years ago, human beings made the crossing on small, rudimentary watercraft. No vessel has survived from this time, but scholars now surmise that the early settlers undertook the voyage on bamboo craft. These people were hunter-gatherers depending on their surrounding flora and fauna for survival, and they settled in coastal environments with abundant sea life. They then proceeded to settle Australia and Buka in the northern Solomon Islands by about 30,000 years ago. A few thousand years later, the early settlers reached the southernmost islands of the Solomon chain and proceeded no further. Increasing ocean gaps separating Near Oceania (Australia, New Guinea, the Bismarck Archipelago, and the Solomon Islands) from Remote Oceania (which begins with Vanuatu) prevented further migration. Over the next 20,000 years, these migrants began settling down and started cultivating yams and taro (Australia, where the inhabitants maintained a hunting and gathering lifestyle, being an exception). With the glaciers receding, Near Oceania became isolated from the rest of Asia and developed a vast array of languages. Near Oceania is one of the most linguistically diverse regions in the world, where not even one percent of the world's population speak almost 25 percent of all human languages. Linguists puzzle over this diversity and call these languages Non-Austronesian to distinguish them from the Austronesian varieties arriving with the second wave of migrants.

Roughly 5,000 years ago another wave of settlement swept into Near Oceania. Archaeologists trace this influx to the island of Taiwan, and the distinctive characteristic of this second expansive phase is a particular type of pottery known as Lapita (named after a site on New Caledonia—an island located at the opening of Remote Oceania). Unlike the much earlier wave, these settlers possessed sophisticated open-water crafts such as sailing outrigger canoes that probably was developed in the calmer waters of Southeast Asia. These settlers spoke a new language group known as Austronesian, which encompasses speakers from Easter Island to Madagascar. The cultural complexity of these migrants is best defined by their distinctive decorated pottery produced with the use of stamps to impress designs before firing. While the migrants came from Taiwan or the Southeast Asian archipelagos, most archaeologists believe that the immediate homeland of the Lapita people, as they are sometimes called, is to be found in the Bismarck Archipelago in Near Oceania. By about 2000 BCE these Lapita colonists braved the water gap separating Near and Remote Oceania or, to be more precise, the distance between the Solomon Islands and Vanuatu. In 1000 BCE they had reached the Fiji, Samoa, Tonga triangle, and the movement came to a temporary halt—possibly caused by increasing distances and the upwind sailing directions in eastern Polynesia. Roughly around the same era, Lapita pottery disappeared from the archaeological record. Over the next 500 years the settlers were busy readying themselves to voyage into the most distant corners of the Polynesian triangle: Hawai'i, Rapa Nui (Easter Island), and Aotearoa (New Zealand). Somewhere between 500 and 1000 CE the settlement of the Pacific Islands was completed. Many believe, however, that the intrepid navigators did not stop there but continued east, on to American shores. While this is most likely the case, Polynesians did not leave a trace as their relative small numbers were probably easily absorbed into existing populations.

TRADITIONAL NAVIGATION AND SOCIAL ORGANIZATION

Traditional navigation relied on several methods. The most obvious is celestial navigation, which engages well-defined sets of star networks at night and the sun during the day. The stars' rising and setting positions provide markers for a cognitive star compass that exists mostly in the mind of the navigator. Ocean currents, indicated by the canoe's movements, can also be employed to set a defined course. An often overlooked technique is "expanding the target." Some of the islands within the navigator's path are tiny in comparison to continental landmasses. In order to avoid missing land in the vast oceanscape, navigators expand its circumference. While physical expansion of the actual landmass is nearly impossible, a skilled navigator uses the daily flight patterns of birds, wave refraction from shore, and the changing water coloring to guide the approach.

Navigation implies a special relationship with the ocean that had a profound effect on social organization. Archaeologists generally concur that the initial expansive Lapita society was a far cry from the later highly stratified societies on Hawai'i and Tahiti in eastern Polynesia. The basic element of stratification may have been inherent already in the settlement process, as the unchallenged authority required by a successful navigator also applied on land. The rich valley slopes of some of the high volcanic islands, for instance in Hawai'i, also necessitated central authority for large irrigation projects sustaining growing populations. Yet even if the high volcanic islands of eastern Polynesia invited societies to settle down, long-distance voyaging continued to play an important role in their development. Historians all too often exaggerate the impact of Europeans on the Pacific Islands, arguing that island communities were relatively self-contained and isolated from each other. Archaeologists add to this theory by emphasizing that cultural development in these societies was essentially an internal process driven exclusively by the urge to adapt to a newfound environment. This concept, however, contradicts Polynesian mythology, which abounds with tales of valiant navigators traveling between distant islands. Moreover, the ocean allowed for a symbiotic relationship between societies on so-called high volcanic or continental islands and those living on relatively smaller coral islets.

It is only recently that historians have paid increasing attention to regional connections between and among different islands. Such was the case of a trade system linking the coast of southeastern New Guinea to the adjacent Massim Islands. Anthropologists have generally focused on the exchange of ritual objects in this area as opposed to the more "common" goods such as foodstuffs and pottery. Recent studies reveal that the

Massim trade lasted at least 2,000 years and was vital for the nutritional diversity of both high (i.e., volcanic) and low (i.e. coral atolls) island societies. A similar relationship also existed in the Caroline Islands in Micronesia, where a long-distance communication network known as *sawei* linked the high islands of the Palauan archipelago and Yap with the low islands over a distance of a little less than 1,000 miles. The island of Yap stood at the center of this exchange system, with its society utilizing important forms of currency, the most important one being the famous stone "money" discs, to forge alliances. Historians evoke images of a "Yapese Empire," where supposedly powerful Yapese overlords extracted tribute from the coral atolls of the Caroline Islands by means of sorcery. Some, however, are quick to point out that this "tribute" involved elaborate gift exchanges and frequent disaster relief following tropical storms in the region. Indeed, anthropologists concur that the inhabitants of the coral atolls benefited considerably from exchanges with the Yapese. For the Yapese, especially those residing in the northern districts, these connections brought less tangible items but more important alliances in times of feuds. Most of the long-distance voyaging from that area was actually performed by the atoll dwellers, which explains why traditional navigation in the Carolines has survived into our century. It was, after all, a master navigator, Mau Piailug from the Caroline island of Satawal, who led a reconstructed double-hulled canoe from Hawai'i to Tahiti in 1976. This not only attested to his navigational abilities, but it also reintroduced navigation to the Hawaiian Islands and partially contributed to a renaissance of indigenous customs and beliefs in Polynesia.

If the Yapese imperial reach was a precarious one, most historians agree that the Tongans established a semblance of an empire shortly before Europeans caught a glimpse of this vast ocean. Archaeological finds and oral traditions speak of an expansion of Tongan power about the year 1400 CE from the island of Tongatapu, first to other islands in the Tongan chain and later into Fiji to the west and Samoa to the east—up to 500 miles distant. The emerging Tongan maritime empire built its strength by placing junior members of the Tongan elite in outlying islands; through strategic marriages they enforced head island Tongatapu's authority. Remnants of this empire existed well into the era of Euro-American imperial dominance in the 1800s. While Tonga exercised authority over distant islands, its imperial reach was quite different from those of the Europeans following the 1500s. Control within the Tongan "empire" rested, much as in the case of the Yapese, on reciprocity. While tribute from Fijian and Samoan isles went to Tongatapu, the Tongan chiefs depended on redistribution of wealth—a concept integral to Polynesian chieftainship. Polynesian mythology includes frequent tales of "evil" chiefs bent on extracting resources, who soon lost their power to ambitious usurpers. Reciprocity was an important way of establishing identity in the realm of the Pacific Islands. Identity based on gift exchange not only provided regional contacts throughout the Pacific, but also created a society that avoided the rigid ethnic categorizations that followed European invasion into the area.

Overwhelming evidence exists to attest to the regional connections among Pacific Islanders. Supra-regional links, however, were absent prior to 1500 CE. There is, for instance, no indigenous name for the area called the Pacific. The most recent division of the region into Near and Remote Oceania derives from archaeological efforts to chart the region according to settlement patterns. Most historians, on the other hand, prefer to use the older division proposed by geographers following the 1700s. The commonly accepted division of the area into Melanesia, Micronesia, and Polynesia has no indigenous origin. Instead, European geographers relied on the Greek language to guide their cartographic fashionings. The most culturally homogeneous region, comprising the triangle between the islands of New Zealand, Easter Island, and Hawai'i, they entitled Polynesia (referring to "many islands"). They continued to name the chains of islands to the north of New Guinea, encompassing the Marshall, Mariana, and Caroline islands, as Micronesia (or "small islands," due to the limited land surface). Last but not least, the largest and most diverse region, encompassing New Guinea, the Bismarck Archipelago, the Solomon Islands, New Caledonia, and Vanuatu, was entitled Melanesia (meaning "black islands" and so named after the inhabitants' skin color). By the 1800s they added Indonesia (the name deriving from the Indian influences of Buddhism and Hinduism that held sway over a large segment of insular Southeast Asia) to provide a convenient link between the Pacific and Asia. In the end, the prerogative of naming the larger geographical features of the region rested with the Europeans who voyaged the Pacific.

A "Spanish Lake": Iberian Journeys to the Pacific Ocean

With the settlement of the Pacific completed by about 1000 CE, two-way voyaging between islands continued well into the 1500s. Europeans followed in the wake of the tremendous accomplishments of the Austronesia settlement, but they did provide the region with a coherence it did not formerly possess. Maritime historians have argued for a long time that the Pacific as a "nexus of global commercial and strategic relations" remains foremost a European construct or artifact.

The integration of the Pacific into a larger global setting was related to developments occurring in the other oceans. The main trailblazers were Portuguese and Spanish, making inroads into Africa, the Americas, and Asia. Searching for the source of Amerindian gold and silver, restless Spanish conquistadors crossed South America until they reached *El Mar Del Sur*. This was Vasco Núñez de Balboa's view of a new "Southern Ocean" that figured as a counterpart to the North Sea, or Atlantic Ocean. Native American legends had accumulated about legendary continents that supplied rulers with endless supplies of precious metals and gemstones. But before the veracity of these accounts could be explored, the Southern Ocean provided an imaginary gateway for the exploitation of Maluku, the spice islands of the Moluccas located at the very edge of the Indian Ocean. Maluku and its spices had long been one of the major focal points in the Indian Ocean world (see chapter 1). Unfortunately for the Spanish, the Portuguese arrived there first. By 1498 they had rounded Cape Agulhas, off the tip of what is now South Africa, and reached the Indian Ocean. A decade later they established outposts in crucial ports there, such as Goa and Melaka. Friendly relations with the sultan of Ternate allowed them to partake in the spice trade of Maluku. The Spanish crown also was interested in the region. By the second decade of the 1500s, its representatives sought to establish a direct route to the trade-rich Indian Ocean through the Pacific.

An expedition in 1519 under the leadership of Ferdinand Magellan tried to investigate the possible passages between the Atlantic and Pacific Oceans and a westerly route to the Spice Islands. Born into Portuguese nobility, Magellan had earned his distinction during Portugal's initial arrival in Maluku. He failed, however, to convince the Portuguese rulers to fund a shorter route to the islands. Magellan consequently transferred his allegiance to Spain and found the Habsburg emperor Charles I eager to support his plans. After emerging from the 330-mile-long strait now bearing his name in South America, Magellan and his crew traversed the new ocean for about 15 weeks without any major incidents. Inspired by the absence of natural disasters in the area, Magellan christened this body of water *El Oceano Pacifico*, adding to a long history of misnomers. Magellan's astonishing feat of missing virtually all major archipelagos until reaching the northern Pacific emphasizes once again the Austronesian nautical accomplishments. Magellan sighted only two uninhabited islands until, on March 6, 1521, the lookout of Magellan's flagship *Trinidad* reported land.

The undernourished and scurvy-ridden crew rejoiced as they pulled into a harbor of the island of Guam. Immediately surrounded by the Chamorro people in their agile *proas* canoes, the Spaniards were the first Europeans to make contact with an Oceanic society. Initial restraint on both sides was soon overcome when the Chamorros helped themselves to Spanish objects, especially iron implements. What the Spaniards interpreted as "theft" may have been the protocol governing drift voyages. Castaways were common in the world of Oceania, and the host society often supported voyagers in need in return for canoes and belongings. The Spaniards, however, had no intention of following this protocol and responded with violence, setting a precedent for many encounters to come. Attempting to illustrate the superiority of their weaponry, the Spaniards initially shot over the Chamorros' heads, but when the captain's skiff went missing, Magellan organized a landing party. When the war party landed on the island of Guam, they looted and destroyed everything in their path. Leaving behind seven dead Chamorros and 40 to 50 burning hamlets, the party returned to the ships with an ample supply of provisions. According to some accounts, they also brought the entrails of the slain Chamorros, which they thought would cure their ailing scurvy victims. This encounter marked the beginning of recorded cannibalism in the Pacific, even if the perpetrators were Europeans and not the often-faulted Pacific Islanders. Magellan also continued the naming tradition his predecessors had started in the Atlantic Ocean. Magellan decided to call Guam and its surrounding islands *Las Islas Ladrones* (Islands of Thieves) due to the so-called thieving nature of their indigenous inhabitants. Magellan left three days after his arrival, but only after kidnapping one Chamorro to serve as navigator and interpreter for the Spaniards.

Magellan continued on to the islands later known as the Philippines, where he made landfall on an island in the Leyte Gulf. While meeting local dignitaries, Magellan did not fail to notice the presence of Chinese silks and weapons encrusted with gold. This seemed to confirm that indeed they had reached Asia and had connected the Americas with this continent. The implements and garments displayed by the indigenous people also suggested that the Philippines were part of a larger network stretching from other regions in Southeast Asia to China in the north. Continuing on to the island of Cebu, Magellan involved himself in the factional politics of the islands. In an attempt to make them friendly to the Spaniards, Magellan attacked their enemies located on the neighboring island of Mectan. The counterattack of roughly 1,500 indigenous men led to a wild retreat of Magellan's outnumbered 50 men. In the ensuing scramble, Magellan met his death, depriving the expedition of its leader. The remaining two ships of the expedition headed southward until they encountered the island of Tidore in Maluku. Ultimately, only one vessel returned to Seville in September of 1522, with a skeleton crew of 18 under the command of Juan Sebastián del Cano. Despite these losses, the voyage was hailed as an instant success. The spices in the *Victoria*'s hull more than made up for the financial losses of the expedition, and it proved that westward navigation from the Americas was indeed possible. The discovery and navigation of the Strait of Magellan alone was a tremendous feat, yet it proved to be so hazardous and difficult to locate that navigators often opted against its use.

LINKING ASIA TO THE PACIFIC: INSULAR SOUTHEAST ASIA

Insular Southeast Asia, located between the Indian and the Pacific oceans, provided a major incentive for Spanish voyages through the Pacific. Its spices and close location to coveted Chinese markets beckoned further exploratory ventures from the Americas. In this process important connections were forged linking the Americas, Asia, and selected Oceanic societies. The European arrival in insular Southeast Asia did not displace the significance of the indigenous societies residing there. Dutch, Portuguese, and Spanish administrators soon learned that political accommodation was just as important as outright military conquest. They had learned this lesson in Africa and the Americas, as earlier chapters illustrated.

Following Magellan's voyage, Spain made several other attempts to reach Maluku by sailing east. Organizing a total of eight expeditions to 1565, the Spanish crown had to accept high costs in silver bullion and human lives. They hit two major impediments to exploration immediately. First, the vastness of the Pacific made exact placement of newly encountered areas difficult, if not impossible. The Spaniards made good use of the astrolabe and the magnetic compass, yet longitude remained an illusive pursuit, bewildering navigators and mapmakers alike. Longitude describes the location of a place on earth east or west of a north–south line called the prime meridian. Unlike latitude, which has the equator as a natural starting position, longitude has no natural starting position. Currently Greenwhich, a district of London, serves as such. Second, the prevailing easterly winds of the Pacific made the return voyage to the Americas a daunting task. Politically too the Spaniards faced disadvantages in relation to the Portuguese. The initial Treaty of Tordesillas (1494; see chapter 2) did not address the Pacific and the coveted Maluku. A follow-up treaty in the city of Zaragoza (1529) placed the islands of Maluku as the easternmost outpost of the Portuguese trading empire in Indonesia. Now effectively barred from Maluku by this treaty, Spanish explorers turned to the Philippines as a major operational base. The islands themselves offered few exploitable resources, but their proximity to China was potentially enriching.

It was not until 1565, with the expedition under Miguel López de Legazpi, that Spain's secure foothold was established in the Philippines. More important was the return voyage to the Americas. With Legazpi effectively preoccupied with consolidating Spanish rule in the Philippines, it fell to his pilot, Andrés de Urdaneta, to return to the Americas. A lucky star guided Urdaneta's endeavor as he sailed high into the north Pacific, catching the prevalent westerlies to guide him home. He had found the *tornaviaje* and thus solved the problem of the return voyage. In the meantime, Legazpi established alliances with key political leaders in the Philippines by treaties that provided a semblance of sovereignty over the islands. The discovery of a natural harbor in Manila Bay on the island of Luzon induced Legazpi to make that his capital.

The founding of Manila in 1571 coincided with the establishment of a galleon ship trade, which brought silver from Acapulco in Spanish Mexico and returned with porcelain and silk from China. Vessels left Acapulco between November and April and followed the trade winds to Manila. They left Manila between May and September, when southwest monsoons sped the vessels northeast to the Japan currents; there they caught the prevailing westerlies, which swept them to a latitude of 40 degrees north. They made landfall in California, a region claimed but little explored by the Spaniards, before continuing on to Acapulco. The eastbound route usually took five months, while the westbound voyage usually took only three months. The galleon trade peaked in the last decades of the 1500s and the first decades of the 1600s. In 1597, the amount of silver bullion sent from Acapulco surpassed the Atlantic trade. The trade network linking China-Manila-Acapulco, and from there across Mexico to Havana and Cartagena in the Caribbean and then through the Atlantic to Seville and other ports of Europe, was to last 250 years, until the sailing of the last galleon in 1815.

The galleon trade for the first time conclusively linked the Americas, Asia, and the Pacific Islands. Vessels carrying silver from the Americas and luxury items from China required a convenient stopover location to replenish the galleons from Acapulco. Magellan's *Islas de Los Ladrones* were such a location. By the end of the 1600s, the Spaniards established a mission frontier in Guam and the surrounding islands, now christened with the more benign name of the Marianas. Initial friendly overtures with the indigenous Chamorros turned sour, and some Jesuits fell to martyrdom.

Spanish retaliations were swift and concluded the conquest of the Marianas within a few years. Disease and the violence of the Spanish conquest reduced the Chamorro population by 90 percent, nearly exterminating them. To minimize resistance, Spanish authorities concentrated the remaining Chamorros on Guam and increased the population of this island with auxiliary migrants from the Philippines and New Spain. The Jesuits made a few attempts to venture outside of the Spanish strongholds, but when these were unsuccessful they concentrated on the evangelization of the indigenous Chamorros.

In comparison to the Portuguese colonial empire called *Estado do India* (see chapter 1), the Spanish involvement in Southeast Asia was rather limited. It was mostly confined to the Philippines and stood under the direct influence of the viceroys of New Spain in present-day Mexico. The Spanish mission in the Philippines had two distinct, yet related, aims. First was the conversion of the indigenous peoples—a religious but also political mission that facilitated trade with China. The Spaniards, much like the Portuguese before them, soon found that their riches depended on the inter-Asian trade. European goods, other than silver bullion, did not find a ready market in Asia, and the trade in the Philippines depended on surrounding countries. The Spanish hold on the Philippines was precarious at best. It was based on a few towns, the capital of Manila being the most important one. The situation was even worse in the southern islands, where indigenous Muslims actively resisted Spanish-imposed Christianity. The support of missions to spread the gospel was a continuous drain on the Spanish treasury; however, the Spanish missions provided a powerful unifying force to the islands. Roman Catholicism served on one hand to consolidate diverse populations; but on the other hand, it strengthened the Islamic hold in the archipelago's southern islands. The tension between Muslims and Christians is still felt in the Philippines to this day.

The Spaniards were not the only ones struggling to establish themselves in island Southeast Asia. The Portuguese may have had an advantage over the Spaniards when it came to Maluku, but they struggled in vain to establish a monopoly over the spice trade in the area. Although they operated out of their fortified emplacement at Melaka, thus controlling the chokepoint of the Strait of Melaka, their encroachment hardly displaced the predominant local traders. In fact, the arrival of the Iberian traders in the region increased the amount of merchandise and demand for local products (i.e., spices). In response, other states began to consolidate. When the Sultanate of Melaka disintegrated after the Portuguese conquest in 1511, a number of states broke away from their former overlords and established independent states. The Portuguese, for instance, were unable to control the growth of the Islamic states of Johor and Aceh, both former holdings of the sultan of Melaka. Not only did these states assert their autonomy, they posed a significant challenge to the Portuguese presence in the region. Throughout the 1500s the rulers of Aceh tried to take Melaka from the Portuguese, partially with the help of troops from the distant Ottoman Empire. Even if Aceh's attempts ultimately failed, such endeavors indicate that Portugal was more on the defensive than the offensive in Southeast Asia.

The economic climate of the 1500s encouraged the centralization of other areas as well. Much as in the Pacific Islands, a number of societies had developed a maritime nomadic lifestyle to trade with the land-based kingdoms on the island of Sulawesi. The best examples of this were the Bugis. In conjunction with the arrival of the Europeans, the Bugis brought considerable wealth to the emerging commercial center of Makassar on the island of Sulawesi. As Makassar grew, it rivaled the European settlements of Melaka and Manila. Makassar's attractive location then aroused the interest of the Dutch. Intervening in local hostilities, the Dutch ultimately managed to conquer the city. Even so, the Bugis traders, refusing to bow to the Dutch, moved on to another location. The adaptation and nomadism of the Bugis is best expressed by the following saying: "We are like birds sitting in a tree. When the tree falls we leave it and go in search of a larger tree where we can settle."

The Dutch were the third European power to venture into insular Southeast Asia. Their arrival in this region was the byproduct of Spain's imperial policies. By 1581, the Netherlands, formerly a subject of Spain, had declared themselves independent. King Philip II's answer to the rebellious Dutch was to cut off their lucrative trade with Portugal. Unwilling to surrender their commercial gains, the Dutch commenced to undermine the budding Spanish–Portuguese trade in the Indian Ocean. Initial attempts to get to the Pacific replicating Magellan's route, however, failed miserably. Crew members arriving in the Spanish-controlled Philippines were executed as pirates. By 1602, after several rounds of negotiations, a new syndicate was formed to strengthen Dutch attempts: the United East India Company (Vereenigde Oost-Indische Compagnie, or VOC). With a full monopoly over trade with the East, the VOC emerged as a powerful competitor for Spaniards and Portuguese alike. It did, however, soon find that the Portuguese, who had made arrangements with local populations, were extremely difficult to dislodge through frontal assault. The VOC thus started to build a system parallel to Portugal's. It founded Batavia, now

Jakarta, on Java and branched out. It established itself in Cape Town, near the southern tip of Africa, and in Ceylon. From their secure bases, the VOC soon started to control most of the European trade in insular Southeast Asia. By 1641, the Dutch conquered Melaka, one of the last Portuguese strongholds in the area. They occupied Mauritius as a slave depot, secured Ceylon and Formosa for their trade, and were granted "favorite nation status" in trade with Japan. Indeed, the Portuguese were left relegated to a few pockets such as Macao, thus effectively ending the *Estado do India*. The Spaniards seldom left the Philippines, which in Dutch eyes had limited economic potential. Despite the arrival of these European parties and the influx of considerable money, none of them replaced the Asian peddling trade, instead operating within it. The new European commercial centers of Melaka, Manila, and Batavia, however, did much to challenge indigenous states in the area. They also served as centers for further expansion.

The Dutch used Batavia for further expansion into the Pacific. Their exploration was purely economic in nature, as VOC officials developed a keen interest in the legendary lands to the south partially sighted by their ship captains. Obsessed with the riches such islands might contain, Dutch governors at Batavia commissioned a number of exploratory ventures. The most important of these was that of Abel Tasman, who in 1642 saw and charted Tasmania, New Zealand, and the archipelagos of Tonga and Fiji. Despite the cartographical significance of such ventures, VOC officials ceased sponsorship of these endeavors, which they deemed too costly.

LINKING ASIA TO THE PACIFIC: THE EAST ASIA CONNECTION

China and Japan also played key roles in the economic integration of the Pacific. While Chinese and Japanese explorers, freebooters, and traders had a tremendous impact on the area of South and Southeast Asia (see chapter 1), both countries actively discouraged outward expansion. The arriving Europeans filled this void and became important go-betweens operating in East and Southeast Asia, providing continuity to the cultural and economic links previously established. European settlements in Southeast Asia, such as Batavia and Manila, attracted Chinese settlements outside their homeland and began the process of China's global diaspora (dispersal).

Chinese merchants clearly desired Southeast Asian trade, but following 1368, the Ming Dynasty enacted a series of trade limitations that was to last until the second half of the 1500s. There was strong bias against any kind of merchants, deriving from Confucian teachings. Regarded as seeking profit rather than human benevolence, merchants found themselves on the bottom of traditional Chinese society, which had more regard for scholars, peasants, and artisans. Despite this ban, the southeastern Chinese provinces continued to trade and settle in *Nanyang* (Southern Ocean or Southeast Asia). China exported silks and porcelain while importing cotton and spices. Chinese and Japanese pirates preyed upon unsuspecting vessels in the South China Sea. The continuing link to Southeast Asia increased in 1567 when Ming officials authorized maritime trade from the southern Fujian province. These officials were less inspired by the search for wealth than by their inability to prevent smuggling and piracy. When the invading Manchus secured northern China after 1644, southern China continued to be loyal to the Ming, which led to a significant drop in trade with Southeast Asia. Once the Manchu-supported Qing dynasty gained the upper hand by the latter part of the 1600s, however, maritime trade once again thrived.

From their bases in India and Southeast Asia, the Portuguese were the first to take advantage of the China trade. Initial missions were unsuccessful, and Ming Dynasty officials issued orders to expel the foreigners. There was, however, a continuing local Cantonese interest in the spices and sandalwood obtained from the new Portuguese enclaves in Southeast Asia. Although Canton was officially closed to foreign commerce following 1522, illicit commerce continued to thrive. In 1550, the Portuguese secured a foothold in Macao. In a mutually beneficial trade, the Portuguese gained access to Chinese goods, in particular silk and porcelain, and the Ming dynasty had a certain degree of control over the new foreigners.

Japan's location in the Pacific provided a major incentive for maritime trade. In the 1500s there were major impediments to economic exchange. China's Ming authorities, the largest market for Japanese silver and copper, treated Japanese merchants as pirates and smugglers and passed edicts limiting trade. The Japanese civil wars of the 1500s also stifled trade. The arrival of the Portuguese, followed by other Europeans in the 1540s, provided respite. The great unifiers of Japan—Oda Nobunaga, Toyotomi Hideyoshi, and Tokugawa Ieyasu—realized the potential of these new arrivals. The Portuguese, hungry for Japanese silver, which they utilized in their trade with China, became effective go-betweens for Japanese trade. Likewise, the Portuguese provided much sought after Chinese trade items, such as cloth, porcelain, and iron. Profits from this trade strengthened the position of Oda Nobunaga and his successors, and the growth of cities gave rise to a wealthy merchant class that invested heavily in foreign commerce.

The unifiers were therefore more enthusiastic in welcoming the Portuguese and their armory than China. Oda Nobunaga took great interest in the arquebus, a Portuguese rudimentary rifle, and had his craftsmen duplicate them. The developing arsenal played a crucial role in the unification of Japan, since at the time of his death in 1582, Nobunaga had brought over half of Japan under his control. However, another introduction by the Portuguese proved more problematic: Christianity. Initially gaining many converts, Jesuit missionaries benefited from the fact that the unifiers of Japan turned a blind eye to their religion. Struggling against powerful Buddhist monasteries in their attempt to gain control over many provinces, the rulers first focused on other threats. This would soon change, however, as Toyotomi Hideyoshi later saw the ascendancy of a new loyalty to the Christian faith; by 1587 he issued an edict to expel all Jesuits. The measures became even more drastic when Hideyoshi's successor, Tokugawa Ieyasu set up a shogunate under his name. Ieyasu regarded Christianity with deep suspicion and feared intervention into his politics. Throughout the early 1600s, Ieyasu banned Christianity and restricted Europeans to a few key cities. His successors went even further. By the 1640s, Japan was a closed country, preventing foreigners from entering and Japanese subjects from leaving the islands. Nagasaki was the sole port accessible to Chinese and Dutch traders—Japan's window to the outside world until the 1850s. The Dutch, as the only Western traders, managed to convince the reigning shogun that their agenda was based entirely on trade, not on religion. They gained permission to settle and trade from Dejima, an island artificially created to keep the "red-haired foreigners" at bay.

The arrival of Europeans in Southeast Asian spawned a Chinese diaspora. The Spanish invited the Chinese to settle in Manila, since they regarded them as a useful minority to construct their settlements. Moreover, Spanish authorities hoped that this would increase trade with the Chinese mainland. The Chinese took the offer and settled in great numbers in the Spanish-controlled cities. By the beginning of the 1600s, Manila harbored 30,000 Chinese, who were deeply engaged in trading silk, textiles, food, furniture, and porcelain. Although many of them did not settle in Manila permanently, their presence greatly outnumbered the 1,000 Spaniards and Mestizos who sought to implement imperial rule in the archipelago. As a result, the relationship between Spanish overlords and Chinese residents was tense at best and was often marked by violence. Threats of a Chinese invasion, real or otherwise, led to several massacres and expulsion edicts to control the explosion of the Chinese community. Ultimately the

Spaniards realized that they could do very little without the Chinese go-betweens; however, relations continued to be strained until the end of the Spanish rule in the Philippines in 1898.

The VOC encouraged Chinese to travel to Dutch-controlled Batavia to assist them in their trading endeavors. The founder of Batavia, Jan Pieterszoon Coen, even wrote: "There are no people who can serve us better than the Chinese." To encourage emigration to Batavia, Coen sent parties to the Chinese mainland to forcefully acquire immigrants. Likewise, he blockaded Manila and Macao to divert Chinese junks to Batavia. Despite these enthusiastic campaigns to encourage Chinese settlement in the Dutch outpost, later governors frequently mistrusted the newcomers, and, much as in Manila, they openly discriminated against the Chinese. Violence and physical isolation, however, did not discourage the Chinese community from flourishing over the next centuries.

GEOGRAPHIC IMAGINATIONS: UNKNOWN CONTINENTS IN THE PACIFIC

One of the main outcomes of Magellan's journey around the world was cartography. European maps, beyond the newly found Americas, had relied formerly on the assertions of the Alexandrian geographer Ptolemy, who in the second century CE argued that the southern ocean was a land-locked entity. Magellan's four-month journey showed the vastness of this new ocean and proved that Ptolemy and others following his lead had greatly underestimated the earth's proportions. This, in turn, provided an avenue for new geographical perspectives.

One shared feature on maps in the 1500s was an austral (or southern) continent. There were compelling intellectual reasons for this. The Flemish master cartographer Gerardus Mercator argued that an austral continent provided a counterbalance to all of the northern lands, without which the world would be destroyed. Budding Spanish geographers made similar arguments. Yet their case for symmetry derived less from a belief in the earth's balance than from conviction of the perfection of God's creation. By about 1530, maps of the earth indicated a continent entitled "Terra Australis Incognita" (Unknown Southern Continent). New Guinea was regarded as either the beginning of this continent or an offshore island. Many of these ideas may have been misinformed, but they provided an incentive for further exploration.

One version saw these unknown lands as the legendary region of Ophir that had provided wealth to the biblical King Solomon. In the Americas,

Spaniards believed that the Incas had indeed reached these islands and had acquired at least part of their riches there. Such accounts propelled the viceroy of Peru to command Álvaro de Mendaña de Neira to search for these islands. His first trip (1567–68) led him to a set of islands, which he called Yslas de Salomon. His stay in the so-named Solomon Islands was marked by violent encounters with the indigenous people and loss of life for both Spaniards and Solomon Islanders. Returning to Peru, he gave utterly disappointing accounts. With no gold or spices to show for the voyage, the viceroy prevented further excursions into the Pacific. Mendaña persisted, however, and by 1595, almost 30 years after his first commission, he obtained permission to sail out again. He took with him a band of settlers to establish a Spanish colony and missionaries for good measure. Unable to pinpoint the location of the first islands he had formerly contacted, Mendaña soon arrived at a larger set of islands in Polynesia he christened the Marquesas, a name they carry to this day. Here too, encounters were less than peaceful: the Spaniards killed an estimated 200 islanders. Continuing on to the Santa Cruz archipelago (part of the Solomon Islands), the Spaniards decided to settle, but disillusionment and violent encounters soon pushed them to abandon the area. Mendaña died there of disease, leaving his lieutenant, Pedro de Quirós, in charge of the settlement. Abandoning the islands, Quirós and the survivors arrived in Manila in 1596. Undeterred by his experiences, Quirós insisted on launching another expedition in search of Terra Australis. By 1605, he obtained royal authorization and sailed with hundreds of settlers to establish a Spanish outpost. Encountering several islands, Quirós finally reached an island in what is now Vanuatu. Thinking he had reached the upper coast of the unknown continent, Quirós named it La Australia del Espiritu Santo (the Southern Land of the Holy Spirit). His settlement, which he aptly named New Jerusalem, was soon under siege from local inhabitants. After several weeks of violent encounters, Quirós abandoned the island and returned to Acapulco in New Spain (Mexico). Disappointed by the failure to discover riches, the Spanish crown desisted from other attempts at settlement and explorations.

Despite the Spanish and Dutch explorations of the 1500s and 1600s, European knowledge of the Pacific beyond the rim of the Americas and Asia was marginal at best. This would all change over the course of the next century. Between 1600 and 1700, the main ocean-traversing powers were Spanish galleons on fixed routes between Acapulco and Manila, with a few surveys by British and Dutch vessels. No permanent settlements came of Mendaña's or de Quirós attempts in the Solomon Islands and Vanuatu. Yet fascination with the Pacific continued unabated. This is

FIGURE 3-2   INDIGENOUS PEOPLE OF NEW GUINEA DEPICTED BY SPANIARDS IN 1606
Source: Reprinted by permission of Archivo General de Simancas.

nowhere better illustrated than in Charles de Brosses's account of the *Histoire des Navigations aux Terres Australes* (History of Navigation in Southern Lands) originally published in 1756 in France. Spearheading a number of speculative accounts in the 1700s, de Brosses's rendition brought together formerly scattered references to Terra Australis Incognita. While still bordering on imaginary renditions of the great unknown, his account nevertheless interspersed scientific motivations alongside pure commercial usages of such a continent. As such, his work clearly marks the beginning of the Age of Enlightenment, which, while heir to commercial exploitations, also suggested the exploration of the Pacific realm for knowledge's sake. The other innovation of this work was the division of the still largely unmapped Pacific into Magellanic, Australasian, and Polynesian domains.

De Brosses's volume signaled the beginning of a new era of exploration. Large-scale expeditions still had as their objectives the general reconnaissance of new islands and their potential for commercial usage. At the same time, however, the expeditions carried "learned gentlemen"—artists and scientists who recorded the flora, fauna, and human societies they encountered.

These studies required government sponsorship and coincided with a general emergence of royal academies of sciences in many European cities.

Strategic considerations continued to play an important part in this endeavor, and the rivalry between France and Britain, highlighted by the Seven Years War (1756–63; see chapter 2) was one of the main forces driving continued exploration. Opening the round of Pacific exploration were Samuel Wallis and Philip Carteret for the British and Louis-Antoine de Bougainville for the French. The highlight was Britain's James Cook, whose three voyages (1768–80) accomplished three great missions: Dispelling the myth of the Terra Australis Incognita, charting major archipelagos in Melanesia and Polynesia, and discovering the Pacific's economic potential. Cook's voyages inspired the British and the French, and reawakened Spanish exploratory quests. It was not until the voyages of George Vancouver (1791–95) that the last of the great mysteries, the existence of a Northwest Passage connecting the Atlantic with the Pacific Ocean, was conclusively laid to rest. The result was a flurry of new maps and interesting tales from Pacific inhabitants that turned Europeans, on the verge of intellectual and political revolutions, into avid readers of the explorers' accounts. By the late 1700s, science reigned supreme in enlightened Europe. Prior to Bougainville's voyage to the Pacific, science was a mere byproduct of navigation and charting. Cook, on his three voyages to the Pacific, carried as many as 15 scientists. His followers, the Frenchman La Pérouse and a Spanish expedition led by Alejandro Malaspina carried many as 20 of these experts. Ships started to resemble floating laboratories. While the Europe of the Enlightenment triggered exploration of the Pacific Ocean, the news returning from these regions continuously fueled new exploratory endeavors.

Science also played a prominent role in charting the Pacific. As much as the Dutch and Spanish explorations of the 1600s had opened the Pacific for European consumption, they were still affected by one major flaw: the determination of longitude. The Spanish and Dutch used dead reckoning to determine longitude and often failed to accurately locate places on maps. By the 1700s, most cartographers knew that longitude was tied to the question of timing. On the surface the basic issue seemed simple. Scientists knew that the earth rotated 360 degrees in 24 hours, and by performing basic calculations they knew that each hour corresponded to 15 degrees. All one needed was to establish a known longitude at one's point of departure and continue to measure time as the ship advanced into the ocean. This simple calculation, however, required near-exact measurement of time. Yet up until the late 1700s even the most accurate clocks were susceptible to the ship's motion and changes in gravity. There were several attempts to remedy this problem. Astronomical occurrences, such as eclipses, were one possibility to measure time, but they were infrequent and required accurate observational instruments. To solve the problem, the Greenwich Royal Observatory developed a Board of Longitude, which made grants for research and awarded prize money up to £20,000. The winner, a London clockmaker named John Harrison, produced a spring-driven chronometer that could meet the demands of the board. The famous version of this timepiece (H4) was introduced in 1759. The second method that came into practice was based on lunar distance, dealing with irregularities of the moon's motion. A German mathematician produced accurate and complete tables of the moon's angular distance and certain fixed stars. Armed with an English translation of the same tables, Cook performed such measurements on the first voyage before switching to the H4 timepiece on his second voyage. The timepiece allowed for the emergence of accurate maps and allowed for a complete charting of the Pacific Ocean in the latter decades of the 1700s.

ENCOUNTERS

TAHITI AND HAWAI'I

One of the places that most impressed European intellectuals was the island of Tahiti. Samuel Wallis and the crew of the HMS *Dolphin* were the first Europeans to sight the island in 1767. The encounter between the two radically different societies during Wallis's stay at Matavai Bay soon erupted into violence. The conflict, partially triggered by the theft of European objects, left many indigenous people dead. Wallis's attempts to claim the island for King George III were soon forgotten, but his final dealings with the Tahitians set a new path for other encounters to follow. Partially intimidated by British firepower, the inhabitants offered Tahitian women to British crew members. This ensured peaceful relations and easy access to desired Western goods. Less than a year after the *Dolphin*'s departure from the islands, the Tahitians spotted the sails of the *Etoile* and the *Boudeuse,* two French ships under the command of Louis-Antoine de Bougainville. This time, negotiating a more difficult anchorage at Hitiaa Bay, the French sailors of the *Boudeuse* were treated to a spectacle:

> The aspect of this coast offered us the most enchanting prospect. We hardly believed our eyes.... All these people came [in canoes] crying 'Tayo' which means 'friend' and gave thousands of signs of friendship. They all asked nails and ear-rings from us. The canoes were full of females, who for agreeable features, are not inferior to European women;

and who, in point of beauty of the body, might with much reason vie them all…. It was very difficult amidst such a sight to keep at their work 400 young French sailors who had seen no women for six months. Despite all our precautions, a young girl came upon the quarterdeck near one of the hatchways, which was open to give air to those heaving at the capstan below it. The girl carelessly dropped the cloth which covered her and appeared to the eyes of all beholders much as Venus showed herself to the Phrygian Sheppard—having indeed the celestial form of a goddess.

Ensuing trade involving European iron nails and Tahitian women continued the pattern encountered by Samuel Wallis and his crew. While the British were markedly indifferent to this trade, the French regarded Tahiti as a carefree society, especially sexually. Bougainville, enthralled by this spectacle, christened the island *La Nouvelle Cythere*, which was more than an attempt to bring Tahiti into western Greco-Roman mythology. Indeed, Cythera, as the classical birthplace of the goddess Venus, created the New Cythera (Tahiti) as a place where European values in the 1700s could be reinterpreted. However, as his carpenter reported the rapid disappearance of nails from his supply and from the ship's structure, Bougainville was quick to leave the island behind.

James Cook, who appeared in Tahiti in 1769, experienced a similar display. Cook stayed at Tahiti for a longer period to perform important scientific observations. Members of the English Royal Society hoped that observing the transit of the planet Venus through the sun would supply important calculations for the establishment of longitude. Less concerned with celestial bodies than with earthly ones, Cook and the "learned gentlemen" soon saw cracks emerging in Bougainville's renditions of paradise. Rather than an island of unencumbered free lifestyle, Tahiti revealed clear class distinctions separating chiefs and commoners.

Despite accounts to the contrary, positive European commentaries on Tahiti grew throughout the late 1700s. Consequently, European intellectuals developed a fond affection for the island and its inhabitants. Philosopher Denis Diderot, for instance, wrote a supplement to Bougainville's voyage where a Roman Catholic priest argues vehemently with a Tahitian individual, only to recognize the defeat of his own values. The priest, in defeat, finds solace in the arms of several female companions, signaling the end of a repressed era. Diderot's account was just one of many philosophical attempts to use stipulated Tahitian cultural models to question European society's rules at the times. The result was that wealthy aristocrats longed to see Tahitians in the flesh. Tahitians were only too happy to oblige, as they had their own questions about European society. The Europeans' sheer insatiable appetite for Tahitian women produced one burning concern for Tahitians: Could it be that European shores abounded with men and had few or no women? Armed with a curiosity that equaled their European counterparts', several Tahitians made the long voyage to the mysterious continent. Unfortunately many died in transit, partially debilitated by the new diseases arriving into the Pacific Ocean. Two famous Tahitians made it to France and Great Britain. Bougainville brought Aotourou to Paris, while Cook brought Omai to London. Both greatly entertained the aristocracy. Encounters with the rulers of the respective countries inspired stories and plays, and it is certain that they drew on their exoticism to explore European women and obtain answers to their queries. In short, these "noble savages" as Europeans called them, made a considerable impression on Europe, much as Europe made an impression on them. The two Tahitians became "tainted": on his return to Tahiti, Aotourou died from an ailment, most likely syphilis, on the island of Madagascar. Omai unfortunately was a victim of his acquisition of European dress and objects; his unwillingness to share them made him an outcast in his home society.

Transformations soon affected Tahiti and the surrounding Society Islands. In 1789 mutineers took over the HMS *Bounty*, a ship captained by William Bligh, whose mission was to retrieve breadfruit from Tahiti for African slaves toiling in the Caribbean. The lure of Tahiti proved too much to handle for many crew members, and they decided to take over the ship. Setting Bligh and his supporters adrift, they tried to recreate the Philosopher's stipulated paradise. Escaping to remote Pitcairn with a number of Tahitian women and men to lead the life of the "noble savage," the mutineers soon saw their lives descend into a hell of bloodshed and despair. Only one of them lived to tell the tale. In their wake, missionaries sought to save what they considered to be a degenerate society and, after initial failure, were instrumental in the creation of the first Christian kingdom in Polynesia. The attention to Tahiti also would make it a ready target for European imperialism, as the French in the 1840s descended on the region to recoup their losses to the British in New Zealand and Australia.

Tremendous changes also engulfed the Hawaiian Islands after the arrival of James Cook. Although there is controversy surrounding the interpretation of Cook's stay in the largest island of Hawai'i, there is agreement that he became involved in important Hawaiian ceremonies. Whether fitting the role of a god or a high-ranking individual (Hawaiian classification is much more fluid than the Judeo-Christian in this regard), Cook played along with celebrations in his honor at Kealakekua Bay in 1779. He complied with the Hawaiian urgings to leave the island at the end of the festivities and headed north to search for the elusive Northwest Passage. A storm sprung one of his masts, however, and Cook was forced to return to Kealakekua Bay only a few days after his departure. The festive atmosphere that greeted him the first time he pulled into the bay was all but gone. An icy reception soon led to Hawaiian "thievery," probably less to procure desired European goods than to test the boundary of a seemingly insatiable supreme being. The disappearance of a skiff right under Cook's nose was too much for the exhausted captain to take, and he opted to organize two shore parties—one to recover the skiff and another one, led by Cook himself, to take high-ranking chief Kalaniopu'u, hostage for the duration of the repairs. A large gathering of Hawaiian warriors foiled Cook's plan for a speedy return to the ship, and violence erupted. While trying to reach safety, Cook was stabbed in the back by one of the daggers his crew had exchanged with the Hawaiians, and was then killed with clubs. Several of his marines shared his fate. The event solidified the memory of one of the world's foremost explorers and gave Hawaiian society a bad name in Europe.

Cook's visit had tremendous implications for Hawaiians themselves. The introduction of venereal diseases caused a tremendous population decline, whose full extent can only be estimated at 50–80 percent over the next 50 years. And while Cook refrained from distributing muskets to Hawaiians, later arrivals eagerly supplied them to chiefs throughout the islands. While certainly not the only factor, firearms were instrumental in the unification of the islands under Kamehameha. An even greater impact was the erosion of the old belief system. With the arrival of Cook's vessels, the *Discovery* and the *Resolution*, Hawaiians began to question some of their cultural values. The ships provided a space outside of island control where the chief's rules were suspended. It is on these ships that men ate with women, defying an important *kapu* (taboo) upheld under the traditional religious system. The ships also allowed commoners to trade with sailors without observing traditional laws. Some historians believe that even if Hawaiians were able to uphold their culture at the advent of Europeans' arrival, the mere presence of a new "lawless space" started a process that would, by 1819, lead to the overthrow of the religious system without the intervention of European missionaries.

CHINA

As noted earlier, European entrepreneurs and monopolizing companies targeted China in their search for wealth. The Spanish and Portuguese had little initial impact on China; the mission effort they supported, however, provided an important intellectual bridge between Western and Eastern traditions. The Jesuits proved to be most successful in this regard. The most famous Jesuit leader was Matteo Ricci (1552–1610), who realized the importance of understanding the intellectual framework of Chinese scholars and dazzled them with new techniques for memorization. He introduced European cartography, enriched with the growing outlines of the Americas, and the new marvels of clock making and astronomical observations. As their cultures influenced each other, Ricci and his fellow Jesuits started to don Chinese clothing, speak Chinese languages, and adapt European world maps to reflect the Chinese world view. Instead of placing Europe at the center of the map, Ricci and others located China in the middle to reflect the Chinese view of their country as the Middle Kingdom (*Zhongguo*, the Center of the Universe). Ricci's efforts of almost 20 years were finally rewarded when the imperial government allowed him to establish a mission outpost in Beijing.

A major point of the Jesuits' acceptance of Chinese culture involved the incorporation of Confucian teachings. Confucius was, for the Jesuits, a teacher and scholar rather than a religious leader. The Jesuits placed much value on the moral issues inherited in the teachings of Confucius, which they regarded as similar to some of their own. Consequently, Confucius's writings were translated into Latin and other European languages. In fact, the very term "Confucianism" does not exist in China, but was invented by the Jesuits and reflected their distinct interpretation of the classics. In this sense, the Jesuits contributed to the emergence of Sinophilism (enthusiastic admiration of things Chinese, deriving from the Latin word *sinae* for Chinese) in European intellectual circles in the 1600s and 1700s. Despite initial success, the Jesuit effort in China fell into decline when disputes among fellow Roman Catholics (predominantly the Dominican and Franciscan orders) led to a reform of the mission effort. Instead of accommodating local religious beliefs, the pope decreed that missionaries were to adhere to official Church dogma. Further disputes between the Roman Catholic Church and Qing officials led to the expulsion of the Jesuits and other missionaries in 1715. The edict was not strictly enforced, as those Jesuits whose expertise included astronomy and cartography could stay behind. Relations remained strained, however, and subsequent Qing emperors placed severe restrictions on Christianity.

Despite the collapse of the mission frontier in China, Jesuit efforts sparked European intellectuals to involve themselves in this region. German philosopher Gottfried Leibniz, for instance, argued that the Chinese surpassed Europeans in the field of ethical philosophy. Leibniz even went so far as to suggest a religious exchange. European missionaries should be encouraged to import revealed religion to China, while Chinese should send missionaries to Europe to teach natural religion.

The main promoters of Chinese culture, or at least the European rendition of such, were the philosophers of the Enlightenment in the 1700s. They attempted to displace Christianity (a religion of revelation) with a deism (a religion of reason) encountered in Chinese models, ironically transferred to Europe by the very missionaries they detested. Inspired by the Chinese, European philosophers argued for a distant God who withdrew from active involvement in human affairs. While still allowing for a divine source of creation, deism permitted inquiring minds of the 1700s to freely investigate the world. God was equated with a watchmaker who had retreated from his creation and left it to human beings to investigate the inner workings of the earth. Not only did Chinese conceptions of the universe inspire scientific endeavors, they also provided ideal types for political leadership. For Voltaire and other prominent European philosophers, China represented the ideal model of the enlightened monarch. In their view, the Chinese emperor ruled by the rational values of Confucianism and was surrounded by a class of scholars elected for their merits rather than birth. Much as in the case of Tahiti discussed earlier, the European understanding of Chinese culture was incomplete. However, China figured prominently in initiating change in Europe's intellectual landscape.

The continuing exchanges between Europe and China also had important implications for the Pacific Islands. Following the large-scale exploratory Pacific voyages, British export trade shifted from India to China. The British East Indian Company had, through a number of favorable peace treaties, gained access to Dutch Indonesian waters and secured a foothold on the Malay Peninsula. At the same time, the loss of the 13 colonies in North America prompted the founding of a convict settlement in newly charted Australia. Despite the convicts' enduring hardship, Sydney developed into an important British port by the 1790s. As European commercial interest in China continued unabated, the Pacific became an important realm for economic resources. Chinese items such as fine porcelain, silks, and tea fetched high prices in Europe. Chinese authorities, however, severely restricted the trade on their end. By 1757, Qing officials declared Guangzhou (Canton) the sole port for foreign trade, with a limited number of merchants allowed to engage in the exchange. Direct contact between the Qing government and foreign traders was strictly forbidden, and diplomatic missions, such as the English mission under Lord Macartney in 1793, were dismal failures. Silver, the main item in demand in China, created a tremendous drain on British national treasuries, until the introduction of opium. Merchants were forced to look afresh at the Pacific Islands in their attempt to locate alternative resources. James Cook initiated this interest when on his failed search for the Northwest Passage the British captain carried North American sea otter and seal pelts back to China. In Guangzhou, his crew realized the value of these items, and a commercial rush soon began to the northwest coast of America to obtain the desired resource. The resulting fur trade (1787–1825) became the prerogative of the young American nation and propelled its expansion to the Pacific. On their long voyages to Chinese shores, the Americans replenished their provisions in the Hawaiian Islands. There, almost by sheer accident, a crew took on bundles of sandalwood for cooking fires. The ensuing demand for this fragrant wood in China, where it had formerly been imported from Southeast Asia, brought many merchants to Hawai'i until the wood was exhausted by 1828. American traders initiated a cycle of debt with Hawaiian chiefs that ultimately resulted in repeated foreign naval interventions and land alienation. With the majority of the Hawaiian sandalwood collected, the demand shifted to other islands, including Fiji, the Marquesas, and, by about 1840, New Caledonia and the New Hebrides—areas that had been charted but not exploited by commercial traders. As the commercial circles in the Pacific widened, new items were added to the exchange. Besides sandalwood and sealskin, bêche-de-mer (also known as the sea cucumber) became a major exchange item in the China trade. The dried and cured meat of this animal was considered a delicacy in China, so traders lost little time in establishing outposts throughout the Pacific to gain access to the valuable resource.

The whaling industry also blossomed in the Pacific in the first half of the 1800s. Whale oil was a crucial resource before the production of vegetable oil and petroleum. The oil was especially valued as an important lubricant and had many applications in the textile industry. The mammals' meat and bones were used as fertilizers in agriculture. Fleets of whalers originating in New England descended on the Pacific Islands, encouraging the growth of prominent port and beach towns such as Honolulu and Lahaina in the Hawaiian island chain. After the sandalwood boom, whaling provided another commercial enterprise for the islands.

Yet the whalers' arrival was seasonal, and crews brought with them numerous social problems (such as venereal diseases) affecting the states of the Pacific.

Before the 1800s, the Pacific had defined integrated subzones, one of which, insular Southeast Asia, provided the link to the Indian Ocean and bridgehead for intrepid Austronesian settlers on their journeys into the heart of the Pacific. Their settlement, which ranks as one of the major historical accomplishments of the area, created further subzones of cultural and economic incorporation. Where Austronesians had led the initial settlement into the vast expanses of the Pacific Ocean, entirely isolated societies became the exception rather than the rule. The dominating integration of the Pacific was a European creation and took a good 300 years to accomplish, much longer than in the Atlantic Ocean. By the 1800s, however, European expansion into the Pacific Ocean had created an arena of encounters that linked American, Asian, European, and Oceanic societies. These encounters shaped all of the societies involved, however, without establishing a clearly dominant leader. By the second half of the 1800s, the balance slowly shifted in favor of Europe and its dependencies. The year 1850 thus provides a convenient cutoff for the narrative of this chapter. Following this turning point, technological innovations as well as scientific and medical breakthroughs would bring about an age of imperialism with tremendous implications for the world's oceans.

CONCLUSION

Humans had ventured into the Pacific expanses since the end of the Pleistocene, but it was ultimately the Austronesian expansion that reached the most distant corners of the Polynesian triangle and presumably the coastal areas of the Americas. This expansion resulted in extensive exchange systems. The close integration of the American and Asian landmasses, however, had to wait until the European intrusion following 1500. Seeking commercial profit, Europeans slowly linked Southeast and East Asia to the island world of the Pacific Ocean and the Americas. Unlike the case in the Atlantic, however, this process took the better part of three centuries, spurred by a search for mythological landmasses. While these were ultimately unsuccessful, the searches led to nautical innovations and geographical knowledge by the last decades of the 1700s. Increasing encounters between radically different societies also produced tremendous cultural changes.

SUGGESTED READINGS

Readings about the Pacific and adjacent areas have proliferated over the last two decades. For a detailed overview on the history of the Pacific Ocean consult the ongoing series edited by Dennis O. Flynn and Arturo Giráldez entitled *The Pacific World: Lands, Peoples and History of the Pacific, 1500–1900* (Brookfield, VT: Ashgate, 2001–). In terms of the history of the original inhabitants of the Pacific Islands, there is Donald Denoon et al., *Cambridge History of Pacific Islanders* (New York: Cambridge University Press, 1997). Denoon also edited a work on *Australia, New Zealand, and the Pacific Islands* (New York: Blackwell, 2000) that looks at the larger context of the Pacific Islands. On the settlement of the Pacific Islands there are a number of prominent works, most recently Patrick V. Kirch, *On the Roads of the Winds: An Archaeological History of the Pacific Islands before European Contact* (Los Angeles: University of California Press, 2000). In this regard consult also Geoffrey Irwin, *The Prehistoric Exploration and Colonisation of the Pacific* (New York: Cambridge University Press, 1992). Paul D'Arcy's book *The People of the Sea: Environment, Identity, and History in Oceania* (Honolulu: University of Hawai'i Press, 2006), is an important attempt to identify larger patterns in Oceanic maritime history. A more traditional and a bit dated account of European Pacific Exploration is J. C. Beaglehole's *The Exploration of the Pacific*, 3rd ed. (Stanford: Stanford University Press, 1966). The reader should also consider O. H. K. Spade's trilogy on European exploration. *The Pacific since Magellan*, vol. 1: *The Spanish Lake* (Canberra: Australian National University Press, 1979) concerns itself with Spanish expansion. The second volume deals mostly with British and Dutch explorers: *The Pacific Since Magellan*, vol. 2: *Monopolists and Freebooters* (Canberra: Australian National University Press, 1983). Eighteenth-century exploratory voyages are explored in the culminating third volume: *Paradise Found and Lost* (Canberra: Australian National University Press, 1988). On the exploration of the Pacific prior to the voyages of the Enlightenment consult Glyndwr Williams, *The Great South Sea, English Voyages and Encounters 1570–1750* (New Haven: Yale University Press, 1997). On the European imaginations of the Pacific Ocean see Bernard Smith, *European Vision and the South Pacific, 1768–1850* (New York: Oxford University Press, 1960). Marshall Sahlins explores James Cook's encounter with Hawaiian society in his *Historical Metaphors and Mythical Realities: Structure in the Early History of the Sandwich Islands Kingdom* (Ann Arbor: University of Michigan Press, 1981) and his *How 'Natives' Think—About Captain Cook for Example* (Chicago: University of Chicago Press, 1995).

Convinced opponent of Sahlins's interpretation is Gananath Obeyesekere, *The Apotheosis of Captain Cook: European Mythmaking in the Pacific* (Princeton, NJ: Princeton University Press, 1992). On Southeast Asia and its role in the nascent Pacific trade consult Nicholas Tarling, *The Cambridge History of South East Asia*, vol. 1: *From Early Times to ca. 1800* (New York: Cambridge University Press, 1992). In this context consult also Anthony Reid's seminal two-volume study on *South East Asia in the Age of Commerce* (New Haven: Yale University Press, 1988–93). On the dual relationship between Europe and China see D. E. Mungello, *The Great Encounter of China and the West, 1500–1800* (Boulder: Rowman and Littlefield, 1999). On the Chinese diaspora consult Gungwu Wang, *China and the Chinese Overseas* (Singapore: Times Academic Press, 1991).

CHAPTER FOUR TIMELINE

1819	First steamship crossing of Atlantic Ocean
1869	Opening of the Suez Canal
1880s	First oil tankers take to the sea
1914	Opening of the Panama Canal
1914–18 and **1939–45**	Two World Wars change the nature of maritime warfare
1960s	First full-blown container ships take to the sea
1982	Law of the Sea Convention establishes Exclusive Economic Zones
1997	The Kyoto Protocol to reduce carbon dioxide levels only partially adopted

CHAPTER FOUR

SEA POWER UNLEASHED: THE WORLD'S OCEANS 1800–2000

GETTING STARTED ON CHAPTER FOUR: How did the steam engine revolutionize ocean travel? How did this invention influence imperial expansion? How did the nature of maritime warfare change from 1914 to 1945? What is the relationship between immigration and ocean travel? How did ocean travel influence the formation of transoceanic identities? What is the relationship between maritime resources and maritime law? What are some current environmental concerns affecting oceans?

CHAPTER OUTLINE

Introduction
Technological Changes: Steamships
Oceans and Empires
    Conquests
    Canals
Sea Power Ideologies and Maritime Warfare
Ocean Liners: From Immigration to Tourism
Transoceanic Identities
    International Women's Movement
    Workers' Internationals
    Pan-Africanism
Shipping Transformations: Oil Tankers and Container Ships
Mineral Wealth and the Law of the Sea
Environmental Concerns
Conclusion

INTRODUCTION

The 1800s witnessed not only the integration of the world's oceans, but also the development of new technologies that would expedite ocean travel and connections. The ensuing breakthroughs facilitated the creation of transoceanic empires and created complex seascapes that increased human migration across the globe. The expansion of imperial powers around the globe between 1870 and 1914 brought about a new sense of internationalism, as well as deepening nationalist sentiments. This chapter explores the emergence of a transoceanic consciousness affecting especially women, pan-Africans, and radical working-class movements known as the Internationals. Entering the 20th century, we will explore the expansion of oceanic warfare and developments affecting transportation of merchandise and passengers. The chapter concludes with considerations affecting the mining of ocean floors and the ensuing legal and environmental implications. While before 1800, individual oceans were well integrated, it was after this date that technological changes brought about the global integration of the world's oceans.

TECHNOLOGICAL CHANGES: STEAMSHIPS

The last three chapters showed that the mastery of the oceans involved constant changes in maritime technology. And while shifts from celestial navigation to temporal measurements of longitude were of tremendous import, few historians deny that the main innovations in shipping technology occurred following 1800, with the introduction of steam. For thousands of years, humans had boldly employed winds and currents to maneuver across dividing waters; steam decreased dependency on these elements.

The application of steam engines for nautical purposes, however, was a lengthy process very much tied to the industrial revolution occurring in Europe. By the second half of the 1700s, steam engines were on their way to replacing animal, human, and wind power in England. Steam engines originally developed to further coal mining soon found their applications in other fields. Steam's main impact was in the field of transportation. Two generations after James Watt's revolutionizing improvements of the steam engine, engineers were developing railroads and steam-propelled locomotives. By 1807, the American Robert Fulton opened steam-powered river travel by introducing the paddle steamer *Clermont* to an expectant public. As the ship traveled on the Hudson River between Albany and New York, the American public enthusiastically embraced this new mode of transportation. Paddle steamers opened North America's vast river systems for exploration and supply. A decade after Fulton's introduction, the number of steamers on the Mississippi and other rivers throughout the United States boomed. Europeans, however, were less enthusiastic about the new invention. The smaller size of their countries made river travel more cumbersome and less economic, and only a few steamers took service on English rivers. Furthermore, launching these ships on the open seas and oceans required tremendous adaptations. The relatively protected waters of the Mediterranean Sea saw a few steamers braving openwater passages. But leaving the sea for the much rougher Atlantic Ocean was a different matter altogether. The result was the creation of hybrid ships that combined the power of steam and wind. The first of such ships to undertake the difficult Atlantic trajectory was the *Savannah* in 1819. While crossing the ocean from the United States to England took 27 days by sailing ship, it took only 4 by steamship.

Three major problems with steamboats became quickly apparent. Using seawater to create the necessary steam for the ship's movement led to dangerous salt incrustations in the boilers, which forced operators to shut down their engines for maintenance, causing costly delays. Similarly, the pounding by relatively high seas caused damage to the paddle wheels, which rendered the steam engines useless. Lastly, early steam engines were hopelessly inefficient as they consumed tremendous amounts of coal. To give but one example, the first ocean liner to cross the Atlantic, the *Britannia* in 1840, had a total carrying capacity of 865 tons. Of this number, 640 tons were reserved for coal to ensure a successful passage, a staggering 75 percent of the entire hold. Such astronomical costs prevented large-scale usage of steamships on the oceans, although they did see increasing service on smaller seas such as eastern Europe's Baltic.

Relevant political events greatly assisted the development of more efficient steamships. The implementation of iron hulls, for instance, was a direct result of naval competition between Great Britain and the United States. Britain came close to ruling the waters after defeating first Napoleon's navy and then the emperor himself; consequently few openly challenged the Royal Navy on the world's oceans. In the commercial realm, however, Britain encountered a powerful competitor in the young and energetic United States. The U.S. had two major advantages: First, a policy of neutrality during the Napoleonic wars had secured access to markets formerly controlled by British and French merchants. Second, while the British Admiralty had depleted British forests in an attempt to keep her merchant and naval fleets afloat during the conflict, the United

States had a seemingly inexhaustible supply of timber, augmented after the Louisiana Purchase of 1803 with the vast expanses of the American West. Following 1815, U.S. merchants were fast closing the gap on civilian shipping, which in turn forced Britain to invest in pig iron. Iron hulls offered a great advantage over wood. For one, iron provided greater safety for the ship, and, as iron could better withstand the stresses of the sea, its use resulted in slimmer hulls with greater speed. This also allowed for greater cargo space, which influenced shipping costs.

At the same time that ships where switching to iron holds, two new innovations also made steamships more efficient. One was the screw propeller, a feature better suited than the paddle wheel to withstand the high seas' pounding. While it provided consistency to the ship's speed, it also made coal consumption more efficient. Efficiency increased with the compound engine, whose cylinders kept demand for coal at an even lower rate. These innovations had two major implications. First, commercial shippers were more likely to invest in steamships than ever before. And second, the ironclad fleet began outdating earlier generations of man-of-war ships, made of wood.

The arrival of these new ships had a tremendous impact on shipping—one of the major results being establishing shipping schedules. While largely unreliable during the age of sails, schedules became far more accurate with the arrival of steam propulsion. The expansion of railways permitted similar developments on land. The schedules of steam locomotives frequently conflicted with local time, generally determined by the position of the sun. Frustrating local differences made railroad officials in England push for a standard time accepted throughout the country following 1840. Such developments were also adopted in the United States and Canada, two countries equally impacted by the expansion of railway lines.

Oceans and Empires

CONQUESTS

Speed not only revolutionized notions of time, but also aided imperial expansion. Steamships, for instance, were instrumental in Britain's defeat of China's Qing dynasty during the conflict known as the Opium War (1839–42). This war is frequently regarded as a starting point for renewed European imperialism. Since the 1700s, the Qing emperors had restricted European merchants to the Chinese port of Guangzhou (see chapter 3). For the better part of a century, Europeans and Americans sought to negotiate better terms with little result. When British East India Company officials introduced opium, a highly addictive narcotic made from the opium poppy, as a contraband item, the unequal terms of trade started to shift. Chinese authorities sought to control the flow of opium by dispatching officials to Guangzhou. When these officials confiscated East India Company opium, British merchants pressured their government into war. This war has been described by observers as pitting a whale against an elephant. The British, with their superior navy, were able to bombard ports and coastal fortifications, but the Qing forces remained too strong to be defeated on land. Following 1840, the arrival of steamships, especially the HMS *Nemesis*, turned the tide. Moving up the vast networks of rivers and canals, British naval forces swiftly defeated Qing war junks and threatened the capital of Beijing. Qing rulers had no other option but to opt for peace. Resulting unequal treaties opened new ports, restricted Qing legal power over foreign nationals, and limited import duties with disastrous effects for Qing rulers. Foreign intervention stimulated further internal uprising against the Qing dynasty. The Taiping Rebellion (1851–64), for instance, devastated entire regions and encouraged massive emigration of Chinese nationals.

Warships also forcefully opened the Japanese islands to Western trade, although the results differed from China. When in 1853 American Commodore Matthew C. Perry steamed into Tokyo Bay, the shogunate granted his demands, which were similar to those imposed on the Chinese following the Opium War. This development, however, set into motion a rapid process of modernization frequently called the Meiji Restoration (1868–1912). The old shogunate was abolished and power returned to the Japanese emperor, with restrictions imposed by a constitution. Over the course of 40 years Japan restructured its economy and borrowed useful technology and knowledge from Western countries. By the turn of the century, Japan was on her way to becoming a naval power. In the 1890s, Japanese forces defeated Qing armies in a conflict over Korea, a war that illustrated both Japan's ability to narrow the technological gap with Euro-American nations and her imperial ambitions. British authorities recognized the rising potential of Japan and signed an agreement with the Pacific nations in 1902 to counterbalance French, Russian, and ultimately German threats in the region. This encouraged further Japansese expansion during the Russo-Japanese conflict (1904–5). The destruction of the Russian Baltic fleet, which had traveled halfway around the world, in the Tsushima Strait in May of 1905 sent shockwaves around the world. Not only did this indicate the impending defeat of a seemingly powerful

European nation, but it also established Japan's might in the Pacific realm. During the First World War (1914–18; see following discussion), Japan furthered its imperial reach by occupying and administering German holdings in China (Qingdao) and Micronesia.

Much has been written about *Pax Britannica*, or British peace, which supposedly reigned over the oceans from 1815 (the end of the Napoleonic wars) to 1914 (the outbreak of the First World War). The Royal Navy was the largest in the world, but its hegemony was challenged by the Americans. America's advantage was its coastline with two oceans, the Atlantic and the Pacific; and while the Atlantic was largely a British "lake," the U.S. concentrated its endeavors on the Pacific and smaller seas closer to its borders, such as the Caribbean. In 1823, U.S. President Monroe proclaimed a famed doctrine urging European powers to abstain from future colonization on the American continents. In fact, the U.S. Navy was hardly in any position to enforce the Monroe Doctrine and was aided by British vessels, who feared other European, especially French and Spanish, intruders. Yet by the end of the 1800s, the United States emerged as a significant naval power and flexed its strength throughout the world's oceans.

CANALS

British and American naval expansion was nowhere more acute than in the construction of two important canals. The first, the Suez Canal (1859–69), highlighted the growing importance of Britain's colony in India. The dream of connecting the Indian Ocean with the Mediterranean Sea was ancient and received additional impetus with the Portuguese trajectory around Africa in 1500. The Portuguese opening of a sea route to Africa only increased the dream of a canal over the next 300 years. The arrival of steam engines made this route much more desirable. Napoleon's engineers were the first to take on this task during their attempt to cut off British trade in the 1790s. But they mistakenly calculated the Red Sea to be 32 inches higher than the Mediterranean, which could have resulted in large-scale flooding of adjacent areas. They consequently abandoned the project. Following generations of engineers realized the mistake and proposed creating the canal in earnest. The political situation in Egypt, however, prevented this undertaking. Finally, a French engineer by the name of Ferdinand de Lesseps received the goodwill of the Muhammad Said Pasha in Egypt and went ahead with the project in the late 1850s. His project resulted in the creation of a new strategic region. British officials soon recognized the importance of the canal and labored hard to take control of the area. The Egyptian ruler's increasing debts allowed them to acquire an increasing portion of the shares, and by 1882 they formally established a protectorate over Egypt to ensure control over the vital lifeline to India. Historians frequently regard British involvement in Egypt to protect the canal as an important starting point for European colonial involvement in Africa (also known as the scramble for Africa).

The Panama Canal (1907–14) illustrated America's rising ambitions. The Frenchmen Lesseps was again involved in the original plans of the canal, but it was the United States that finished the construction. When the U.S. displaced Spain from its last possessions in the Caribbean and the Pacific during a brief conflict in 1898, the path was open for a period of imperial expansion. Over the next three years, U.S. officials annexed Puerto Rico in the Caribbean, as well as Guam, Hawai'i, and the Philippines in the Pacific Ocean. Cuba gained its independence, but experienced increasing American involvement following 1901. The Spanish–American war made the U.S. a Pacific as well as an Atlantic power. This two-ocean vision coupled with the need to ferry troops and ships between the Atlantic and the Pacific oceans propelled President Theodore Roosevelt to intervene in the region. Roosevelt was a firm believer in a strong American navy. He actively supported the construction of the canal through financial investments and negotiations with Colombian officials over the acquisition of land rights. When Colombian officials refused to continue their negotiations with Roosevelt, the American president suggested the creation of a new country. His idea was placed in practice by New Panama Canal Company officials, who encouraged local officials to declare independence from Colombia. Roosevelt backed Panamanian rebels with U.S. marines, thus enabling the creation of the sovereign nation of Panama. In return, the United States obtained a lease of a canal zone ten miles wide for perpetuity. The Panama Canal illustrated the United States' rising involvement in imperial affairs. Such ambitions were also linked to increasing naval conflicts on the world's oceans.

SEA POWER IDEOLOGIES AND MARITIME WARFARE

The expansive moves inherent in canal construction were supported by an ample supply of ideological literature on sea power. The most important theoretician in this regard was the American Alfred Thayer Mahan (1840–1914). Mahan wrote extensively on the rise of Great Britain and her navy, a branch of the military he greatly admired. Far from an abstract exercise in historical writing, however, Mahan believed his studies to provide important lessons for naval warfare in the 1900s. Mahan, as a naval officer who had served on several U.S. vessels, maintained that sea power was the key to world dominance. While this demanded a large fleet of battleships and coaling stations for supply, Mahan also emphasized the need for increased commercial shipping. To support both naval and commercial forces, Mahan advocated the establishment of overseas bases and colonies. Mahan envisioned future naval engagements to be decided by large-scale battleship deployments.

Mahan's influence on global naval buildups was significant. Theodore Roosevelt devoured Mahan's works as he directed his sights to the Panama Canal. In a newly formed German nation Emperor Wilhelm II furthered the development of his imperial navy by ordering copies of Mahan's work to be placed on each German battleship. Likewise, the Japanese government made sure that translations of Mahan's work were available for officers' training schools.

Naval races are frequently regarded as one of the main causes of the First World War. No other vessel symbolized this more than the British HMS *Dreadnought*. Launched in 1906, she soon outclassed all other battleships before her. Most important, her oil-fired turbines could outrun her coal-fired opponents. Ten 12-inch guns provided overwhelming firepower. Commissioned by the British Admiralty to deter the Germans from their massive naval buildup, it instead provided a much welcomed incentive to the continental nation. German officials now had a tool to narrow the gap between the British and German navies, and they shifted their battleship program to accommodate the new ship. The combined construction effort of these battleships, however, could not hide the fact that the two world wars resulted in different naval encounters than predicted by Mahan.

World War I (1914–18) pitted the so-called Central Powers (German and Austria-Hungary, later Bulgaria and the Ottoman Empire) against the Allies (initially Britain, France, and Russia, with more powers joining in as the conflict continued). Most of the significant campaigns were fought on land, most importantly along the western front, a long strip of trenches stretching from the English Channel to the Swiss border. Very little movement occurred along this front over the four long years of intense fighting.

The war also had a significant maritime dimension. The transportation of thousands of British and French colonial troops from Africa and Asia aided the Allies' general war efforts. Likewise, an effective British blockade prevented German colonial troops from Africa and the Pacific from reaching the western front. While hopelessly outgunned, German colonial troops still managed to engage the Allies in a number of campaigns in Africa (most significantly German East Africa) to prevent further deployment of colonial troops. The most telling employment of colonial troops was during the Gallipoli campaign (1915–16) in Turkey. As the western front ground to a halt, the British Admiralty took aim at what they regarded as the weakest link within the Central Powers: the Ottoman Empire. Organizing the largest amphibious operation since the Ming dynasty's efforts in the early 1400s (see chapter 1), the Admiralty had to call upon a large contingent of soldiers from Australia and New Zealand, another result of an increasingly interconnected oceanic world. Known collectively as the ANZAC (Australian and New Zealand Army Corps), they received their baptism of fire during the Gallipoli campaign. While the campaign ended in a disastrous withdrawal of Allied troops, the Commonwealth nations in the Pacific still celebrate ANZAC Day (April of each year) to commemorate the event.

Besides serving as highways to transport troops to the European and Middle Eastern theaters of war, the oceans also became fierce battlegrounds. The Atlantic Ocean and North Sea saw frequent action during this conflict. At the beginning of the First World War (August 1914), the Royal Navy effectively blockaded the German fleet and ports, causing increasing hardships among the civilian population. Besides one indecisive engagement during the Battle of Jutland (in May of 1916), the two fleets had few hostile exchanges. Instead warships targeted commercial shipping. At the onset of the war, German surface raiders successfully thwarted British shipping in the Atlantic and Indian oceans. When the Royal Navy started to dispatch more of her ships in affected areas, German raiders were sunk or effectively neutralized by the end of 1915. More important were German submarine operations against the British Isles. By February of 1915, the German admiralty established a counterblockade involving both allied and neutral shipping. They had to suspend their actions when the sinking of the liner *Lusitania* caused an outcry among the American public. As German offensives on the western front ground to a halt, unrestricted submarine warfare was once again declared in February 1917. Within three months, German U-boats (the term derives from the German *Unterseeboot*) came close to holding Britain captive—in April 1917, for instance, 870,000 tons of Allied shipping was sunk. When German U-boats targeted U.S. merchant ships, the U.S. entered into the conflict. With the shifting of important surface vessels from the Pacific to the Atlantic oceans through the Panama Canal, U.S. military units intervened by establishing convoy systems that paired up merchant ships with naval escorts. Commercial ships once again reached Britain and France safely, and the influx of U.S. soldiers into France turned the tide on the western front.

The interwar years saw an increasing transformation of naval warfare. While submarines and merchant marine vessels continued to play an important role in future conflicts, developments in aircraft carriers were most noticeable. The idea of constructing aircraft carriers to serve as an extension of air power into the world's oceans predated the First World War. During the Great War, the Royal Navy employed some aircraft-carrying vessels against Central Powers targets with limited result. Development of such vessels continued after the conflict, and by the 1920s a number of ships with a full-length flat deck emerged. The Washington Naval Treaty, which placed restriction on the tonnage of battleships in 1922, prompted the conversion of many naval units into aircraft carriers. By the outbreak of the Second World War, the aircraft carrier became a prominent unit in many navies around the world

The Second World War (1937–45) pitted the so-called Axis powers (Nazi Germany, Fascist Italy, and Japan) against the Allies (most significantly Britain, the Soviet Union, and the United States). Besides the important Atlantic theater, Japan's actions in Asia and Oceania opened another maritime front in the Pacific Ocean. In the Atlantic Ocean, there was little change from the First World War. German surface units were no match for the Royal Navy, and confrontations were minimized. German submarines, on the other hand, operating from captured French and Norwegian bases, were successful in harassing Allied shipping. Although quickly organized into convoys, merchant ships frequently lacked escort vessels, and the German admiralty prearranged U-boats into wolf packs with devastating effects. In November 1942, German submarines sank 725,000 tons of allied shipping, seriously threatening British supply lines. Increased protection from escort vessels and aircraft carriers, including innovations in radar and sonar, provided an important breakthrough. By 1943, the battle of the Atlantic was lost for the Germans as U-boat losses soared.

In the Pacific theater, naval operations were even more prominent. The lethal use of aircraft carriers was illustrated in December 1941 when the Japanese navy dealt a devastating blow to the American Pacific Fleet stationed in Pearl Harbor, Hawai'i. Fortunately, the fleet's three American carriers were not in the harbor and soon intervened in the conflict. Amphibious operations brought many areas in Southeast Asia and Melanesia under Japanese control. Then the war turned. While again few direct encounters between battleships occurred in the Pacific, the new aircraft carriers had tremendous impact on the war. First at the Battle of the Coral Sea (May 1942), which effectively halted further Japanese advances into the South Pacific, and then at the Battle of Midway (June 1942), where four

Japanese carriers were sunk, the effectiveness of aircraft carriers became obvious. Equally devastating were American submarine attacks on Japanese commercial shipping. Because the Japanese admiralty deemed the action cowardly, naval officials did not organize their merchant ships into a convoy system, marking them as easy targets. Japanese bases in the Pacific were equally hard hit. The names of Guadalcanal, Iwo Jima, and Tarawa are but a few famed places that experienced fierce fighting. The outcome was always the same, as Japanese garrisons fought virtually to the last man; their passing became known by the euphemism "crushed jewels" to the Japanese public. To avoid the inevitable, Japanese officials ordered their super battleships, such as the *Yamato*, to engage American forces. They never came close to their objective as they were sunk by carrier-based American aircraft. With battleships replaced by aircraft carriers, the Age of the Battleship had effectively ended, and Mahan's predictions about sea power needed adjustments.

OCEAN LINERS: FROM IMMIGRATION TO TOURISM

The ocean had served as a liquid human battleground for centuries, but more important was its function as a route of transportation. Until the arrival of jet aircraft, ocean travel represented the largest means of passenger transport. By and large, the 1800s were marked by a vast migration, either voluntary or involuntary, from Africa and Europe to the Americas across the Atlantic, and from Asia to the Americas and Oceania via the Pacific Ocean. Trips of a more leisurely variety emerged at the turn of the century, and by 1950 most people used ship travel solely for recreational purposes.

The transatlantic slave trade (see chapter 2) was the largest migration in human history to about 1840. After that date, Europeans surpassed that number as, between 1820 and 1930, 50 million individuals left their continent looking for new shores. Historian Alfred Crosby called their new places of settlement "Neo-Europes," because, while separated by thousands of miles from the European continent, they were all located in similar latitudes. Argentina, Australia, Canada, New Zealand, South Africa, and the United States are all located in the earth's temperate zones. These regions had plants and animals that differed greatly from those in Europe, yet their climates allowed for an introduction of European flora and fauna. In short, these regions permitted the export in part or whole of a European environment. Labor designed to tend to this environment was procured elsewhere.

Historians specializing in immigration take two major variables into consideration: "push" and "pull" factors. Immigrants leaving their country

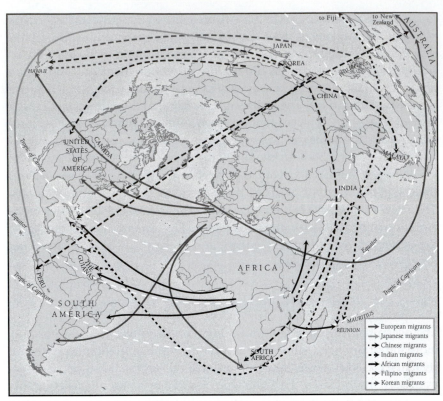

FIGURE 4-1 OCEAN TRANSPORT AND MIGRATION DURING THE 19TH AND 20TH CENTURIES

Source: Used with permission from Traditions and Encounters (2nd ed.), by Jerry H. Bentley and Herbert F. Ziegler. Copyright 2002 by McGraw-Hill.

of birth usually have encountered adverse conditions: Famines, droughts, unemployment, overpopulation, and war all play an important part in urging individuals to emigrate. The pull factors emerge at the place of destination, pulling immigrants into an economy that demands their employment. In the 1800s the greatest push factors affecting Europeans were religious persecution (affecting Jews, especially in Russia), famines (Ireland and southern Italy), and general poverty (eastern regions of Germany). Political unrest and war also influenced migrations in Asia. The weakening of the Qing dynasty in China due to external (Opium Wars; see the beginning of this chapter) and internal (Taiping Rebellion) events persuaded many to migrate overseas. In Japan, the dwindling stability of the Tokugawa shogunate encouraged many citizens to search for new horizons. India also experienced migration. British colonialism increased after 1850, causing many Indian citizens to leave, but the British connection also offered migrants possible means and destinations, in the form of colonies. Trinidad in the Caribbean Sea and the Fiji islands in the Pacific Ocean are examples of places where people from South Asia make up the majority or near majority of island residents.

In the early 1800s, postal service increases established some of the first transatlantic liners connecting North America with the European continent. Most of the ships involved in these services were fast sailing ships known as clippers. The time for passage under sail took somewhere from 4 to 10 weeks, depending on weather conditions. Following the 1820s, a new commodity was added to the regular trade—immigrants. There were two general pull factors in the Americas. Besides the occasional short-lived mineral exploitation (such as the 1848–49 California Gold Rush), rapid industrialization, coupled with an expanding infrastructure (i.e., railroads) contributed to the demand for immigrants in North America. Caribbean and South American need for immigrant labor resulted from the abolition of slavery (as it occurred, for instance, in 1838 in the British colonies of the Caribbean). To prevent the closing of economically vital mines and plantations, a new system was introduced: indentured labor. This labor system involved a contract (ranging anywhere from three to five years) that was binding for both employer and employee. Southern Europeans, especially Italians and Portuguese, were affected by this new system. Yet Indians and Chinese bore the brunt of this new labor practice. Long trajectories across the Pacific Ocean took twice the time of an Atlantic passage, and appalling ship conditions raised mortality rates to 25 percent (or similar to numbers in the early years of the transatlantic slave trade). Common mistreatment and frequent contract violations made life unbearable for East and South Asians alike. The coolie trade, as it was called during this time period, thus resembled slavery in more ways than one.

On the transatlantic side, conditions were slightly better. While European immigrants often experienced harsh treatment from liner crew members considering them little better than commodities, they rarely encountered the same atrocities as Asian voyagers. Similarly, the shorter passage across the Atlantic Ocean also ensured lower mortality rates. But ship disasters were indeed frequent, and lifeboats became a luxury usually reserved to officers and crew members. Food and water often went stale during the passage, and when hatchways were closed during stormy seas, passengers staying below deck fell victim to diseases. Three major illnesses took their toll on these long journeys: cholera, dysentery, and typhus (aptly called ship's fever). Mortality rates on Atlantic crossings started to approach those of the transatlantic slave trade prior to abolition.

Steam power proved beneficial in this regard. Initial hybrid and full-steam liners were prohibitively expensive for immigrants, who continued to prefer sail over steam as an affordable means of transportation. It was the Inman Line, under a combined American and British ownership, that introduced lower fares for immigrants in 1852. Other steamship lines followed suit, and by 1855, steam began to overtake sail as an important market. By the 1870s, the dreaded passage across the Atlantic had been reduced to two weeks, and an increasing number of companies competed for immigrant passengers. The Cunard Line, for instance, chose safety and frugality over speed and luxury. The White Star Line, on the other hand, reversed this equation as her steamers frequently competed over the desired prize of the fastest crossing: the Blue Riband of the Atlantic (awarded 1838–1952, after which the aircraft made ships' speed irrelevant). By the end of the century, these American and British steamers were in competition with German liners, especially the Bremen-based Norddeutsche Lloyd. Increasing liner service also meant a widening rift between poor and wealthy passengers. Rich individuals usually stayed in the plush accommodations of the cabin class, while less fortunate individuals stayed in a long row of bunks under the main deck known as steerage. The survival rate of steerage-class passengers was lower, partially due to the crowded breeding grounds for diseases and partially because few precautions were taken for their safety. This is best illustrated by the famed shipping disaster of the White Star liner *Titanic* in April 1912. After the ship rammed an iceberg, 1,502 passengers and crew members died in the icy seas. Nearly 97 percent of the women and children and 32 percent of the men in the first class were saved. In third class, the survival rate fell to 42 percent and 16 percent respectively. The Titanic too had raced to obtain the coveted Blue Riband, leaving one contemporary commentator to write that the victims "were sacrificed to the greedy Goddess of Luxury and her consort the Demon of Speed." The *Titanic* disaster became a catalyst for new maritime regulations. In the winter of 1913–14, delegates to a conference on Safety at Sea convened in London. Wireless communication became mandatory after it became obvious that most ocean liners employed this service to provide wealthy passengers with news and stock quotes. Furthermore, the wireless section had to be manned 24 hours a day. The conference also mandated the increase of lifeboats and rafts on ocean liners.

The main impact on ocean travel, however, derived less from safety considerations than from immigration limits. In the United States, the Chinese were one of the first ethnic groups to be singled out by anti-immigration laws. Chinese nationals arrived in large numbers in California as a consequence of the Gold Rush and railroad construction. By the 1870s, they became a main target for riots. When California legislators considered banning their entrance into the state, the federal government reacted. The Chinese Exclusion Act of 1882 banned these nationals for 10 years. By 1892 the act was extended another 10 years, and by 1902 Chinese immigration was halted completely. Japanese were also affected by similar sentiments. When Californians wanted to stamp out what they regarded as a "Japanese menace," President Roosevelt intervened and negotiated a gentlemen's agreement with Japanese authorities in 1907. If Japan would deter emigration of its nationals, U.S. authorities would prevent discrimination against the already existing Japanese population. The U.S. Congress further curtailed immigration in 1924. The Natural Origins Act shut off Asian immigration completely and limited European immigration to 2 percent of each nationality residing in the Union. Australia and New Zealand also actively resisted Asian migrants. Their relatively close proximity to China and Japan raised concern about massive numbers of Asian immigrants overrunning the essentially Anglo populations. Initial restrictions of Chinese and Japanese nationals created Asian restriction bills in both countries. Although those bills stood in clear violation of British agreements with Japan, Australia and New Zealand officials continued to show their degree of independence by establishing Immigrant Restriction Acts (1899 in New Zealand and 1901 in Australia) to limit Asian immigrants. Immigration restrictions remain paramount in many countries, especially in Australia.

This essentially reduced immigration to a trickle and forced steamship companies to react. To make up for the shortfall, liners quickly converted their steerage class to a tourist class and opened the door to a lucrative hospitality business. The tourist business enabled the liners to stay afloat for an additional three decades, with a war-related recess between 1941 and 1945. By 1958, however, air travel slowly caught up with sea travel, and by the 1960s it eclipsed it altogether. From the 1980s onward, however, liners made a glorious comeback as cruise ships. As the ocean giants could not compete with the airplane, company officials decided to invest their resources in the leisure industry. The Mediterranean and Caribbean seas became prominent locations for cruise ship tourists. Shipping officials from the Cunard Company (now owned by American cruise group Carnival) even revived the transatlantic cruise with the construction of the largest and most luxurious ocean liner ever: the *Queen*

Mary II. Twice the size of its Long Beach–based predecessor *Queen Mary*, this new vessel came into service in late 2003 and promises to revive some of the past glory of the liners.

TRANSOCEANIC IDENTITIES

INTERNATIONAL WOMEN'S MOVEMENT

Oceans did not serve only as waterways for international imperial control; the same tools that connected the large transoceanic empires of the New Imperialism also enabled people critical of imperial thought to organize on an international basis. Three of these movements are investigated in considerable detail: the Pan-African movement, which sought to unite people of African descent throughout the world; the women's rights movement, which strived for female voting rights and electoral participation; and Socialist International's attempt to provide radicalism with an international platform.

In the late 1800s, several movements emerged demanding equal voting rights for women. These suffrage movements emerged out of a general sentiment to support the abolition of slavery. When many male delegates of the World's Anti-Slavery Convention of 1840 in London opposed women's participation, a number of potential women participants, most notably the American Elizabeth Cady Stanton, chose to engage themselves in an equally noble cause, resulting in the famed Seneca Falls Convention. Leading American and British suffragists went on speaking tours, raised money for the cause, and, perhaps most importantly, organized conventions. The emergent net of transoceanic relationships soon showed results. Discussions surrounding women's suffrage also crossed the Pacific and became a heated topic in New Zealand and Australia, both regions with a substantial European population. Arguing that New Zealand could lead the way in the British Commonwealth, legislators introduced a women's suffrage bill into parliament in 1887. By 1894, women gained the right to vote in New Zealand, followed closely by the new Commonwealth government of Australia in 1902.

These developments in the Pacific ignited the transatlantic suffrage movements. In March of 1888, the U.S. hosted the opening of the International Council of Women in Washington, D.C. While the majority of the more than 3,000 delegates hailed from the U.S., there were several hundred from Great Britain and other regions. Despite their agreement on many central themes, a gulf between American and British delegates was emerg-

ing. American suffragists were mostly nonpartisan, while British supporters were very much engulfed in the liberal politics of their country. Despite
such differences, exchange of ideas continued across the Atlantic, especially after lawmakers ignored frequent requests for the right to vote. A
number of congresses and conferences on both sides of the Atlantic, however, could not prevent an increase in the gulf. In 1906, the Women's Social
and Political Union (WSPU) moved its headquarters to London. With this
move also came a change in strategy. The WSPU became more sensational
in its methods, engaging in violence and hunger strikes to obtain their
goal. While 1909 is commonly seen as the height of the transatlantic suffrage movement, when the WSPU suspended their militant actions for
about two years to create a rapprochement, the gulf widened. American
women became known as suffragists, in other words, moderate or constitutional advocates of women's suffrage, while their British counterparts
became the suffragettes, or those who used militant aims in the accom-
plishment of their goals. The war accentuated the gap; however, the labor
of the transatlantic women's movements finally bore fruit. In January 1918,
the U.S. House of Representatives passed a constitutional amendment
granting women the right to vote. The very same day, the British House of
Lords passed its women's suffrage clause. The developments in the United
States and Great Britain illustrate the importance of transoceanic connections and experiences shared by women's suffrage supporters around the
world.

WORKERS' INTERNATIONALS

Oceanic seascapes also played a crucial role in the creation of international
workers movements. Ever since Karl Marx and Friedrich Engels had ended
their *Communist Manifesto* with the famed words, "Workers of the World
unite," there had been efforts to bring about an international organization
that could stem the rising tides of capitalism, nationalism, and imperialism. The First International (1864–76) was just such an attempt. According
to the founding members, capitalist expansion had reached international
proportion and had created a transnational economy that had adversely affected workers around the globe. The emergence of the First International
in England was an attempt to raise workers' consciousness by providing a
platform from which to address and combat the excesses of the capitalist
system. Early successes of the International included securing voting
rights for English urban workers and successful fundraising for strike support. It further proclaimed that workers should adhere to the doctrine of

pacifism should national wars engulf their individual countries. The use of militancy was suggested only to further the struggle of the working class.

In all of its aspirations at internationalism, the First International remained a European affair, with minority participation from newly industrial nations across the Atlantic. As such, the International was soon embroiled in ideological conflicts that pitted Karl Marx against the anarchists under Mikhail Bakunin. Fearful of Marx supplanting one authoritarian rule with another, originating from the working class, Bakunin rejected many of Marx's arguments. While Bakunin was soon excluded from the First International, Marx was facing opposition from other quarters, which included trade-unionist and moderate socialists. To avoid further dissent, Marx shifted the headquarters of the International to New York. While this ultimately led to the dismemberment of the organization, it also invited transoceanic participation.

The so-called Second International emerged in 1889 in Paris at the 100th anniversary of the French Revolution. It was from the very beginning a much more transoceanic organization than the first, since it included delegates from Australia, Japan, New Zealand, South Africa, and the United States. The Second International focused its attention on the increasing militarization of European nations and called upon workers to stand firm against the agitations of their individual countries' leaders. This renewed emphasis on pacifism also included major statements against rising global imperial ambitions. Yet by and large, members of the International shied away from supporting African and Asian national ambitions against strong imperial powers. This prevented increasing non-European membership in the organization. Short-term success resulting from the outbreak of a first global depression (1873–96) provided the impetus for the main goal of the organization: the avoidance of war benefiting the capitalist world. When the time came, however, to make good on these pledges, many delegates faltered. When global war threatened to erupt in the summer of 1914, supporters of the Second International raised their hands and voices to approve war loans and credits in their respective national parliaments instead of calling for national strikes against the impending slaughter. That August, the Socialist International faltered amid a sea of nationalist sentiments.

An increase in transoceanic participation came with the establishment of the Third International in 1919. Following the successful Bolshevik Revolution (1917) in Russia, Vladimir Lenin decided to use the revolutionary fervor brewing in Europe following the Great War to promote international revolutions. He recognized that the peace conferences in Paris left many people under European imperial rule clamoring for liberation.

Departing from Marx's doctrine that capitalism had to take root before a full-fledged working class emancipation could occur in the colonial world, Lenin argued that a strong centralized vanguard party run by trained revolutionaries could ensure working-class rule. He thus invited participation from colonial peoples to his Communist International (known as Comitern) congresses. Lenin acted more out of a sense of self-preservation than of commitment to the colonial cause. The emphasis on colonial peoples resulted from the general failure of communist revolutions throughout Europe. The waning years of World War One led to the collapse of three empires: Austria-Hungary, Germany, and Russia. Based on Lenin's lead in Russia, two revolutionary movements emerged in Germany and Hungary. A weak democratic German regime was able to quell the communist Spartakus uprising under the leadership of Karl Liebknecht and Rosa Luxemburg only by resorting to military elements returning from the western front. Similarly, a communist regime established by Béla Kun in Hungary succumbed from allied intervention. Attracting young colonial subjects to the inherent internationalism of the communist cause, Lenin could distract European attention away from intervention in emerging Soviet Russia, especially through the support of counterrevolutionist elements. Lenin therefore placed the colonial issues at the forefront during the second Comitern Congress in 1920. Inviting members from China, India, Indochina, and other Asian nations, Lenin hoped to export revolutionary ideas to the colonies. His attempts, however, were soon threatened when emerging communists in colonial dependencies created alliances with an emerging middle class. While Lenin did not witness revolutions in his lifetime, he did nevertheless lay the seeds for successful uprisings in China and Indochina following the Second World War.

After Lenin's death in 1924, the Comitern soon came under the control of Joseph Stalin, who stifled the Comitern's internationalism. Clashing with Leon Trotsky, who wanted to continue the international tendencies of communist movements, Stalin argued that socialism needed to be strengthened in one country (i.e., the Soviet Union) before the revolution could successfully be carried across the borders. While Stalin would ultimately abolish the Comitern in 1943 to allay his American and British allies' fear of international communist revolution, Trotsky fled the Soviet Union and went across the Atlantic Ocean to Mexico. This country, beset by revolution throughout the early 1900s, provided a stage for Trotsky's call for a Fourth International in 1938. Supported by such artists as the muralist Diego Rivera and his wife, Frida Kahlo, Trotsky sought to revive the successes of Lenin's Comitern. Stalinist agents ended Trotsky's life in 1940, but the Fourth International promoted communist movements throughout Latin America—the germination of which would emerge after the Second World War. Communism, like feminism, had become an international and transoceanic movement.

PAN-AFRICANISM

Pan-Africanism is a general term used by historians to designate various transoceanic movements in Africa, the Americas, and Europe that sought to promote unity among peoples of African ancestry. It sought to counter Western discrimination and imperial expansion in Africa. Pan-Africanism had its roots in the abolitionist movements that engulfed the Atlantic world in the late 1700s, and involved people of African ancestry joining Christian people of European ancestry in their denouncing of the African slave trade. An additional incentive came from the shared experiences of white oppression by Africans. The result was not only the abolition of the slave trade by Britain and France in the early 1800s, but also the establishment of two important settlements along the West African coast: Sierra Leone and Liberia. Starting in the late 1700s, American and British philanthropists paternalistically argued that the development of Africans could not be obtained within the discriminating contexts of the Americas. They thus purchased land for the settlement of freed slaves, an endeavor that ironically received additional assistance from U.S. slaveholding states' legislators, who saw freed slaves as a nuisance. The New Imperialism provided further impetus when many European nations grabbed for land on the African continent. The Berlin Conference (1884–85) sought to provide a semblance of lawfulness to this endeavor and sanctioned the European imperial acquisition of Africa. Liberia and Sierra Leone served as ports of entry not only for returnees from Europe, as well as North and South America, but also for African American missionaries who sought to forestall the common European argument that Africa was home to backward peoples.

These imperial developments gave rise to two separate yet related concerns forming the backbone of the Pan-African movements. The first concern argued that the slave trade that had deprived Africans of their freedom had also robbed them of a common identity. The invention of this common "African" identity was key, especially in light of ongoing segregation and discrimination against African Americans in the New World. The second concern argued that imperial dispossession in Africa made unity difficult, if not impossible. The establishment of a united independent Africa was thus at the center of many Pan-African movements. The same steamships responsible for the exploration and ultimate conquest of Africa also connected the continent with dispersed Africans throughout the world. Personal letters and newspapers created an avenue within which to express critical voices. The first Pan-African congress met in London in 1900, with little initial result other than bringing together representatives from Africa, Europe, and the United States.

The first decades of the twentieth century saw two quite contrasting approaches to Pan-Africanism emerging in the U.S. W.E.B. DuBois (1868–1963) was an intellectual who believed that African Americans should strive for civil and political equality. He called upon the African-American elite to assist other less fortunate individuals. His insistence on bettering the living situation of African Americans ultimately led to the establishment of the National Association for the Advancement of Colored People (NAACP) in 1909. DuBois's attempts to better the existence of African descendants from within American society were vehemently opposed by Marcus Garvey (1887–1940), who argued for African separatism. Garvey, a Jamaican native, argued that African descendants lacked knowledge of and pride in their heritage and were thus easy prey to white racism. He held that only a return to Africa could provide a solution. His Universal Negro Improvement Association (UNIA), which he founded in 1914, promoted the slogans "Back to Africa" and "Africa for Africans," which became popular among Pan-Africanists. UNIA and Garveyism grew significantly in the U.S. and the Caribbean. Garvey's main business venture in 1919 was the creation of an international steamship line for commercial and passenger travel, which he aptly named Black Star Line (in response to the famous White Star Line, whose *Titanic* sank in 1912). Garvey's views gained importance through the *Negro World*, a newspaper that had wide circulation and was read on both sides of the Atlantic, including, much to the dismay of European imperialists, in many regions of Africa. Problems soon emerged, however, when mismanagement of the Black Star Line led the U.S. federal government to investigate UNIA. Already worried about his separatist aspirations, federal agents indicted Garvey on mail fraud. Convicted, Garvey went to prison until his sentence was commuted in 1927, but he had to leave the U.S. for good.

The popularization of Garvyism throughout the Atlantic world assisted the Pan-African movements. In 1919, for instance, DuBois called a congress paralleling the Paris peace treaties concluding the Great War. He argued, along with many delegates, that President Wilson's principle of self-determination was applicable to Africa also. The resolution of this congress asked for Africans to participate in government—a resolution that imperial authorities flatly ignored. Consequently, when DuBois called for another congress in 1921, the resolution became stronger, emphasizing a general criticism of American and European imperialism and racism. Again, imperial powers turned a deaf ear—in contrast, however, to the African people who started to attend DuBois's congresses in increasing numbers. The most important congress occurred in Manchester in 1945, following the Second World War. Many future African leaders in attendance (such as Ghana's Kwame Nkrumah) listened to DuBois's call for autonomy and independence. From this congress forward, the center of gravity for Pan-African activity shifted to Africa, culminating in the creation of the Organization of African Unity (OAU) in 1963. DuBois himself renounced his U.S. citizenship and settled in newly independent Ghana (whose national flag added a black star at its center honoring Garvey's movement), where he died the very same year.

Besides official congresses and organizations, Pan-African consciousness also entered popular culture. On the island of Jamaica, Garvey's prophecies inspired a movement known as Rastafarianism. With its belief that the Ethiopian Emperor Haile Selassie (1893–1975) was a divine being, the Rastafarian message spread mostly through the reggae music of Bob Marley (1945–1981). Marley's music and lyrics are partially responsible for spreading Pan-African messages to other people suffering under imperial rule. While Garvey's "Back to Africa" message could hardly inspire peoples throughout the Pacific Ocean area, for instance, reggae music certainly has made an impact on indigenous Hawaiians and Maori (of New Zealand). Both of these Polynesian peoples felt that reggae music spoke to their plight, which involved the loss of sovereignty and ultimately land to Euro-American invaders. Not only have many Maori sported fashionable "dreadlocks," a sign of rejection of Western society and a reconnection with one's cultural roots, but Hawaiians coined a new musical style—Jawaiian—which merged Hawaiian with reggae music. If Pan-Africanism united the Atlantic Ocean in the early 1900s, then reggae music is responsible for taking anti-imperialist messages onto global oceans and airwaves of the late twentieth century.

SHIPPING TRANSFORMATIONS: OIL TANKERS AND CONTAINER SHIPS

The world's oceans have long played a leading role in the transportation of goods and commodities. In the 1960s passenger travel shifted from the oceans to the air; however, transportation costs for air travel continue to be prohibitive for bulk items. Consequently, merchant fleets are now divided into two major categories: oil tankers and container ships.

With the growing importance of oil in the late 1800s, the safe transport of this vital liquid became a major consideration. Transporting oil first began with leaky barrels, which made their loading and passage cumbersome and dangerous. First experiments with tankers—ships designed for the sole purpose of oil transport—were slow in developing. Two major security issues arose immediately. The liquid created unbalances in the ship due to shifting weight in heavy seas; and temperature fluctuations induced expansion and contraction of the flammable liquid. This meant that shipping companies had to make uneasy choices. A tank not filled to capacity, might prevent an unwanted expansion of the liquid in hot weather, but also created a clear stability hazard during a rough passage. Similarly, a tank filled to capacity provided stability, but the expansion of oil in warmer climates could breach the tank or, in the worst case, the hull. Heinrich Riedemann, a German oil importer, tackled this problem by introducing a ship with several tanks. Connected to an overflow system, the tanks could be filled to capacity, and a ventilation system removed hazardous gases. Riedemann's tanker, created in the 1880s, served as a model for future tankers, whose size grew in correspondence with the demand for oil. The demand was fueled by the development of aircrafts and automobiles in the civilian and military sector; the discovery of rich deposits in the Persian Gulf region met most of it. Transportation of oil from Southwest Asia to North America and Europe witnessed a sharp increase. By 1900 only 109 vessels traversing the oceans were tankers (amounting to less than 2 percent of commercial shipping), but the figure had risen to over 6,000 by 1990 (or more than 30 percent of commercial shipping). The 1920s saw America with a clear lead in the oil tanker business, especially after Britain's merchant fleet suffered considerable losses during the First World War. After the Second World War, competitors emerged. Greece and Norway started to invest heavily in the expanding oil transportation industry, and names like Aristotle Onassis became synonymous with the wealth deriving from this trade. Taking advantage of lower tax rates and registration fees offered by Central American or African countries, many shipping company owners opted to fly different national flags. Shipping owners' national "flight" to maximize profit illustrated another important development affecting the last decades of the 1900s. Companies were less and less associated with nation-states, and investments in oil tankers were some of the first endeavors in a sprawling transnational capitalism.

The introduction of container ships was equally transforming to the world of shipping. Up to about 1950, the handling of cargo had changed little since the Age of Sail. Steam introduced a reduction in shipping schedules, but as loading and unloading was performed mostly manually, ships frequently spent more time docked in a harbor than on the open sea. The increasing demand for materials during the hostilities of the Second World War, however, increased experimentation. The best idea for cargo handling originated with an American trucking company owner. Malcolm McLean's idea was simple. Instead of hauling cargo manually onto the ship, workers would arrange the merchandise in a container that would then be lifted entirely onto the vessel. Not only was this solution time efficient, but it also allowed for additional storage room. If arranged properly, for instance, containers could handle ten times the cargo of traditional ships. The containers themselves could be transported to the ship via rail or truck, thereby providing additional time savings. For the process to work smoothly, however, containers had to be standardized across national borders. This was no easy task, and it was not until the late 1960s that the first full container ships appeared on the world's oceans (employing either 20- or 40-foot standardized containers). By the beginning of the 1970s, container ships carried the lion's share of overseas trade. This shift signified again the eclipse of traditional shipping powers. By 1914 Great Britain produced approximately 60 percent of all ships, but the number fell to less than 4 percent in 1977. As containers reduced the amount of labor and time needed to load a vessel, additional problems presented themselves. Port authorities, for instance, had to adjust quickly to the demand of these new ships. This required new infrastructure and investments. Unable to compete with new port installations, several older ports fell into oblivion, while other cities meeting the challenges increased their business. Similarly, the livelihood of longshoremen, the people involved in the loading and unloading of ships, was threatened by the introduction of containers. Negotiations and strikes slowed down the process of employment loss, but ultimately many jobs were lost to the new innovations.

The emergence of tankers and container ships is a sign of a novel process known as transnational capitalism. Emerging multinational companies disassociate themselves from nations by establishing multiple bases throughout the world. Transnational companies thrive on the existence of tax-free havens in the Caribbean Sea and the Pacific Ocean. For the past three decades this new form of capitalism has given rise to considerable conflict and grievances, especially since some of these companies have operating resources that parallel or surpass the national budgets of many countries.

MINERAL WEALTH AND THE LAW OF THE SEA

From 1950 onward, the oceans became more than a mere transportation highway to shuttle raw materials and manufactured goods between continents. The wealth inherent in the sea became a major issue. For thousands of years, people had extracted fish from the sea, but few had declared outright monopolies over a liquid territory. Even the late 1400s (chapter 2) division of the Atlantic Ocean into Portuguese and Spanish spheres was illusionary. As conflict over fishing rights and commercial shipments became more acute in the 1600s, Hugo Grotius, a young Dutch legal scholar, argued for the general freedom of the sea. Grotius perceived the seas' resources, which he understood to be mostly fish, as inexhaustible, and therefore thought they should be free for all. His compatriot Cornelis van Bijnkershoek elaborated on Grotius's writings a century later. Van Bijnkershoek agreed that the sea should be a free domain, but argued for the establishment of an extension of a country's territory into the ocean. He suggested using the range of a coastal cannon, something he estimated at approximately 3 miles, as a measure for territorial waters. Many countries adopted this interpretation in a rather liberal fashion, and some extended their territorial waters to 4 and even 10 miles. Nevertheless, military raids notwithstanding, this rule of thumb was accepted by many navigating nations.

Problems emerged, however, with the discovery of mineral wealth in the oceans. The ancients already suspected copious amounts of resources in the seas' waters. The first attempt at exploration originated with the Germans, who at the end of the First World War were looking for innovative ways of paying their war debts to the Allies. The German South Atlantic Expedition sampled seawater between 1924 and 1928. Unfortunately, the quantities of suspended gold were less and the effort to obtain it was more than expected. The endeavors were consequently stopped. Interest in the ocean basins emerged again through the discovery of rich oil deposits. Offshore drilling occurred already in the 1890s. But it was not until 40 years later that drilling platforms ventured into the open ocean. Wartime need for petrol increased prices, and soon the United States operated several drilling stations in the Gulf of Mexico and off the

California coast. Recognizing the problem of territoriality, President Truman proclaimed in September of 1945 that the United States had the exclusive right to exploit the resources of its surrounding continental shelf. This proclamation was soon followed by those from Mexico and other Central and South American countries. Clearly, international discussion was required to solve this issue. Consequently, in the 1950s, a newly formed United Nations took a closer look at the law of the sea.

Compounding the problem was the location of manganese nodules on the oceans' floor. As the study of the oceans increased, aided in part by the development of anti-submarine warfare, scientists discovered the oceans' floor to be littered with these nodules. Their analysis revealed high quantities of manganese, as well as other minerals such as copper, iron, and nickel. The most astonishing insight was that the concentration of these minerals was higher on the ocean floor than on any part of the continents.

Two major problems prevented the immediate exploitation of these resources. First, the technology to retrieve the nodules was costly and ineffective; second, industrialists feared that a massive exploitation of these minerals could bring about a drop in mineral markets. While the possibility of seabed mining was still being discussed, several newly independent nations voiced concern about the possible exploitation of these resources by Western industrial nations. Cautionary talks soon gave way to conferences. The most important of these was the Law of the Sea Convention (1982). Delegates of this convention determined the width of territorial waters to be 12 miles. Similarly, coastal nations obtained a so-called exclusive economic zone (EEZ) amounting to a 200 mile offshore radius for their commercial exploitation. While unable to interfere in the freedom of navigation, coastal nations obtained all rights to minerals and fish within the EEZ. This convention, ratified by most nations (the United States government finally accepted its provisions in 1994), meant that one-third of the world's oceans were now under continental control.

Environmental Concerns

The location and exploitation of maritime resources, both animal and mineral, brought with it important environmental considerations. Extraction technologies of the 20th century have proven Grotius wrong— the oceans' resources are indeed finite. Some scientists, and more recently historians, see a reversal in the relationship between humanity and oceans. If by 1900 humans still regarded the seas and oceans as a major threat to life and property, over the course of this past century humans emerged as a major threat to the sea.

Fishing was one of the first industries to experience these insights. While whaling in the 1800s drove many whales to the brink of extinction, it was in the next century that smaller varieties of sea life witnessed a similar impact. By 1950, the fishing industry introduced powerful trawlers, which used advanced technology not only in catching the fish but also in locating the shoals. While increasing the yields of fishing, these advances also began depleting the global stock of fish. The rich grounds of mackerel and herring in the North Sea, for instance, propelled much competition in the 1500s and served as one of the incentives for Atlantic expansion. By the 1970s, however, new technology used in fishing had so depleted the stock that the entire area had to be closed down from 1977 to 1981 to allow for fish reproduction. Similarly, the effect of overharvesting fish may increase long-term damages to the food chain, affecting people all over the globe for generations to come.

Pollution is another factor greatly affecting the world's oceans. Chemical pollutants, plastics, sewage, and agricultural runoff can adversely affect the world's oceans. In mild cases such pollutants enter the food chain and ultimately return to the human body via the consumption of fish. Once consumed, the pollutants can be the cause of uncontrolled cellular growth (i.e., cancer) and miscarriages. In the worst case scenario, entire populations of fish die off, thus creating widespread famines around the globe. The pollution of seas and oceans also contributes to prolonged algal blooms along coastal areas. While periodical algal blooms were not uncommon throughout history, certain areas, such as the North Sea, see about 15 percent of the surface covered by the intruder, indicating a clear alteration of the ecosystem. Enclosed seas experience this problem more than open oceans. The transport of dangerous substances adds to environmental degradation. Oil tankers and platforms are a further source of major hazards. Spills and accidents can cover many hundreds and even thousands of square miles of oceans and beaches with a terrifying "black tide," suffocating animal life and preventing fishing.

The latest threat to the oceans, and in return to human life, is the so-called greenhouse effect. Simply told, it involves rising temperatures in the earth's atmosphere, leading to a slow but steady melting of polar icecaps, and consequently to a rise in oceans' water levels. While there is a considerable debate whether these increases in temperature are indeed human caused, many scientists now agree that the accumulation of CO_2 (carbon dioxide) in the earth's atmosphere is tied to the increasing burning of fossil fuels since the industrial revolution and a concomitant deforestation campaign affecting the world's last rainforest reserves. As the atmosphere's carbon dioxide levels increase, it retains more of the sun's heat, consequently melting the icecaps. In December 1997, 160 nations met in Kyoto, Japan, to address the issue. The outcome was the so-called Kyoto Protocol, in which industrial nations agreed to gradual reduction of emission levels during the 2008 to 2012 period. In March 2001, fearing interventions with business practices, newly elected American President George W. Bush announced his opposition to the protocol.

Ironically, the main impact of global warming can be felt by those very countries that benefited immensely from the Law of the Sea Convention. Many Pacific Island nations increased their economic potential through the increase of their EEZs. Rising sea levels, however, threaten their very existence. The nation of Tuvalu serves as a case in point. Located about 600 miles north of the Fiji Islands, the total land surface of this nation is a mere 26 square km (or ten square miles). Tuvalu's EEZ, on the other hand, amounts to a whopping 910,000 square km (or 350,000 square miles). The highest elevation of the archipelago is about 5 meters (or 15 feet), creating an acute awareness of global warming among the 11,000 inhabitants. The government of Tuvalu has repeatedly pointed out that rising sea levels have already contaminated some of their soil and have thus impacted the agricultural output of the nation. Prime Minister Koloa Talake planned in 2002 to join the republics of Kiribati (located in the Pacific) and the Maldives (located in the Indian Ocean) in a lawsuit against the United States and other countries ignoring the Kyoto Protocol, at the International Court of Justice in the Hague. The suit floundered, however, when Talake lost his reelection bid the same year. Even if successful, the suit would have had only limited impact, given the United States' reluctance to accept the international court's jurisdiction.

Epeli Hau'ofa, a Tongan writer, once wrote: "Conquerors come, conquerors go, the ocean remains, mother only to her children. This mother has a big heart though; she adopts anyone who loves her." Hau'ofa wrote these lines in the early 1990s to reflect on the economic and intellectual impact of Euro-American imperialism. The conquerors of the first decade of the 21st century, though, are less characterized by expansive nation-states and are a great deal more threatening than the New Imperialism's steamships. The relationship between humans and the oceans has undergone drastic changes. Human societies seem no longer in awe of the ocean world and are emerging quickly as its main menace. Hau'ofa anthropomorphizes the ocean as the mother of humanity; increasingly, however, as her children are turning away, her heart begins to shrink. EEZs have now attached political boundaries to oceans, and the technology to exploit the resources is sure to follow. Unfortunately, the first to experience the ocean's wrath will be those societies, like Tuvalu, that have had a longstanding relationship with the sea.

CONCLUSION

Technological advances in sea travel furthered linkages among the Atlantic, Indian, and Pacific oceans. Steam engines reduced the dependency on winds and currents and greatly reduced the time required to cross the oceans. Technology also enabled the establishment of artificial links, such as the Suez and the Panama canals, speeding up connections among the world's oceans. Such tools enabled the expansion of European powers, whose fleets were soon joined by others in an attempt to secure increasing sea power. Conflict over oceans grew to global proportions and turned the watery expanses into important theaters of conflict during the first and second world wars. Control over ocean lanes also encouraged migration on an unprecedented scale, which changed the global demographic makeup. Migrations also contributed to the emergence of transoceanic identity formation that greatly affected the 20th century. Ocean integration awoke a concern over maritime boundaries that became particularly accentuated because of the availability of offshore resources. The exploitation of such resources brings environmental concerns into sharp focus. Humans may have mastered oceans over the last two centuries, yet they are now also the source of oceans' main pollution. Similarly, the burning of fossil fuels triggers the rising of sea levels and a possible increase in the number and potency of natural disasters associated with the world's oceans. Hurricane Katrina's devastation of New Orleans and surrounding areas, as well as the increase of hurricanes affecting North American and Caribbean regions in 2005, illustrates the existence of forces that go well beyond human control. It further underscores the point that regional environmental discharges are very likely to have global consequences in the not so distant future.

SUGGESTED READINGS

Daniel Headrick aptly explores the relationship between technology and imperialism in his *The Tools of Empire: Technology and European Imperialism in the Nineteenth Century* (New York: Oxford University Press, 1981). His chapters on steamships (1, 2, 8, and 9) as well as on the building of the Suez Canal and its implications (10 and 12) are of much use for an oceanic perspective on the New Imperialism. Michael Adas takes this analysis further by providing a link between technology and imperial ideologies in his *Machines as the Measure of Men: Science, Technology, and Ideologies of Western Dominance* (Ithaca: Cornel University Press, 1989). Several books dedicated to individual oceans or seas have chapters dedicated to the advances of the nineteenth and twentieth centuries, in particular David Kirby and Merja-Liisa Hinkkanen, *The Baltic and the North Sea* (New York: Routledge 2000), and Paul Butel's *The Atlantic* (New York: Routledge, 1999). Those interested in military engagements on the open ocean over the last two centuries should consult the following: John Piña Craven, *The Silent War: Cold War Battle beneath the Sea* (New York: Simon and Schuster, 2001) and Clark G. Reynolds, *Navies in History* (Annapolis: Naval Institute Press, 1998). The last work traces the development of navies back to antiquity. For a good review of transatlantic suffrage movements prior to 1914, consult Patricia Greenwood Harrison, *Connecting Links: The British and American Woman Suffrage Movements, 1900–1914* (Westport, CT: Greenwood Press, 2000). For a novel view of women's movements throughout the British Empire consult Ian Christopher Fletcher, Laura Nym Mayhall, and Philippa Levine, eds., *Women's Suffrage in the British Empire: Citizenship, Nation, Race* (New York: Routledge, 2000). Stimulating perspectives on international socialism can be found in Stephen Eric Bronner, *Socialism Unbound*, 2nd ed. (Boulder: Westview Press, 2001). A standard work on the Socialist International remains Julius Braunthal's monumental *History of the International*, 3 vols. (Boulder: Westview Press, 1967–80). A very informative narrative on the Pan-African movement, which contains also the connections to the Third International, remains Imanuel Geiss's *The Pan-African Movement: A History of Pan-Africanism in America, Europe, and Africa*, trans. (New York: Africana Publishing, 1974). For an adaptation of Mahan's concept of sea power to the late 20th century consult Luc Cuyvers, *Sea Power: A Global Journey* (Annapolis: Naval Institute Press, 1993). For a succinct overview of important global migrations and their cultural implications consult Robin Cohen, *Global Diasporas* (Seattle: University of Washington Press, 1997). There is a large number of works on ocean liners; one of the most accessible ones is Terry Coleman's *The Liners: A History of the North Atlantic Crossings* (New York: G. P. Putnam's Sons, 1978); the same author also published the noteworthy *Passage to America* (London: Huterinson and co, 1972), which chronicles European emigrants in the 1800s. Maritime law and its implications are best explored in James Wang's *Handbook on Ocean Politics and Law* (Westport, CT: Greenwood Press, 1992). For a recent overview of the early debates on oceanic law consult Mónica Brito Viera, "*Mare Liberum vs. Mare Clausum*: Grotius, Freitas, and Selden's Debate over the Seas," *Journal of the History of Ideas* 64, no. 3 (2003): 361–77. Tuvalu's fate was discussed in a recent issue of the *Smithsonian* 35 (August 2004): 44–52.

✦ INDEX ✦